A POCKET COMPANION TO PMI'S

PMBOK® GUIDE

(UPDATED VERSION)

Other publications by Van Haren Publishing

Van Haren Publishing (VHP) specializes in titles on Best Practices, methods and standards within four domains:

- IT and IT Management
- Architecture (Enterprise and IT)
- Business management and
- Project management

Van Haren Publishing offers a wide collection of whitepapers, templates, free e-books, trainer material etc. in the **Van Haren Publishing Knowledge Base**: www.vanharen.net for more details.

Van Haren Publishing is also publishing on behalf of leading organizations and companies: ASLBiSL Foundation, CA, Centre Henri Tudor, Gaming Works, IACCM, IAOP, IPMA-NL, ITSqc, NAF, Ngi, PMI-NL, PON, The Open Group, The SOX Institute.

Topics are (per domain):

IT and IT Management

ABC of ICT
ASL®
CATS CM®
CMMI®
CoBIT
Frameworx
ISO 17799
ISO 27001
ISO 27002
ISO/IEC 20000
ISPL
IT Service CMM
ITIL®
MOF
MSF
SABSA

Architecture (Enterprise and IT)

Archimate®
BIP / Novius
GEA®
TOGAF®

Business Management

BiSL®
Contract Management
EFQM
eSCM
ISA-95
ISO 9000
ISO 9001:2000
OPBOK
SAP
SixSigma
SOX
SqEME®

Project Management

A4-Projectmanagement
ICB / NCB
MINCE®
M_o_R®
MSP™
P3O®
PMBOK® Guide
PRINCE2®

For the latest information on VHP publications, visit our website: www.vanharen.net.

PMI Netherlands Chapter

A Pocket Companion to PMI's

PMBOK® Guide

(updated version)

A quick introduction to
'A Guide to the Project Management Body of Knowledge'
(PMBOK® Guide)
"PMI," "PMP," and "PMBOK," are registered marks for
the Project Management Institute, Inc.

Paul Snijders PMP
Thomas Wuttke PMP
Anton Zandhuis PMP

Van Haren
PUBLISHING

Colophon

Title:	A Pocket Companion to PMI's *PMBOK® Guide* (updated version)
Series:	PM series
Authors:	Paul Snijders PMP Thomas Wuttke PMP Anton Zandhuis PMP
Reviewers:	Alfonso Bucero (PM Consulting) Portfirio Chen (PM Consultant) Iain Fraser (Project Plus Ltd) Alfred J. Howard (PM by Pros) Crispin Piney (PMI France Sud) Ray Riedel (HP USA) Rodney Turner (Lille University) Thomas Walenta (IBM Industrial Sector, Automotive & Electronics North)
Text editor:	Steve Newton
Publisher:	Van Haren Publishing, Zaltbommel, www.vanharen.net
ISBN hard copy:	978 90 8753 697 8
ISBN eBook:	978 90 8753 961 0
Print:	First edition, first impression, March 2012 Second edition, first impression, March 2012 Second edition, second impression, October 2012
Layout and type setting:	CO2 Premedia, Amersfoort - NL
Copyright:	© Van Haren Publishing, 2012

Contents

Preface

"I don't believe in miracles; I count on them!" Delivering projects successfully is more than coincidence and the success of one individual. It requires project management knowledge by all stakeholders and some well defined processes to ensure real cooperation and drive, in order to make these 'miracles' happen. A relatively small change in the mind-set and actions of all project stakeholders will bring a large improvement in successful project delivery. With this pocket companion to PMI's *PMBOK® Guide* we want to foster this change.

If you are already familiar with the *PMBOK® Guide*, the title of this book 'A Pocket Companion to PMI's *PMBOK® Guide*' is setting your expectations. However, if the *PMBOK® Guide* hasn't crossed your path yet: The *PMBOK® Guide* (*A Guide to the Project Management Body of Knowledge*) is widely recognized as the worldwide standard in project management, confirmed by the fact that more than two million copies are in circulation. However, this rather voluminous standard was lacking an easy accessible and short introduction. This did not facilitate an easy adoption by a wider audience. This pocket guide is intended to fill this gap by creating a straightforward introduction and high level summary of the *PMBOK® Guide*.

This pocket edition is especially useful for project sponsors, project managers, and project team members, as these are the three key roles we distinguish in this book. It is also useful when acting in a project supporting role (for example as a member of a Project Management Office, PMO). It will support all project stakeholders in two ways:

- Better understanding of their role in projects based on good practices in project management;
- Improvement of an organizational-wide project management approach.

At the organizational level it allows for a structured and well supported lifecycle-driven project approach, as well as ensuring all project stakeholders are speaking 'the same language'. It will improve the practical application of project management processes, when these are understood by all and consistently applied. The flexibility of the concept enables all organizations and project teams to adapt it to their level and needs, often referred to as 'lean project management'.

This is exactly what the Project Management Institute (PMI) aimed for when issuing the *PMBOK® Guide*. It has become the international de-facto standard in project management. Many project management methodologies refer to this standard. It is recognized as an ANSI standard for project management processes. Other global standards tend to follow the same direction. The *PMBOK® Guide* is, therefore, a fundamental input when working on projects and striving for project success.

Research confirms that organizational excellence in project management brings clear tangible benefits. We encourage you, your project management community and project stakeholders collectively, to become familiar with the *PMBOK® Guide's* knowledge and processes in order to reap and increase these benefits.

November 2009,

Paul Snijders, PMP
Thomas Wuttke, PMP
Anton Zandhuis, PMP

Chapter 1
Introduction

1.1 Purpose of this Pocket Companion to PMI's *PMBOK® Guide*

This pocket companion to the *PMBOK® Guide* is intended as a brief reference to aid in quickly understanding the purpose, background and key elements of the *PMBOK® Guide.*

What is the added value of the *PMBOK® Guide*? The *PMBOK® Guide* is recognized worldwide as a foundational reference for the application of project management knowledge and good practices. Research has confirmed that it clearly enhances the successful delivery of projects. Project environments that consistently apply this fundamental project management good practice approach not only show better project performance in terms of lower costs and shorter delivery times. They also show higher customer satisfaction. So there are a lot of benefits to gain from its application.

When working in a project management environment, which is far more dynamic than 'normal' operations, good communication is essential. For this you need 'one common language' within your project management environment, which is understood by everyone involved. This pocket guide aims to quickly establish a shared vocabulary and terminology on the project management fundamentals and create a common understanding about the basic project management processes and the key roles and responsibilities.

What is it not? It is definitely not a 'project management recipe book'. The project manager and the team remain ultimately responsible for deciding what good practices shall be applied to the specific project at hand, closely cooperating with the project sponsor and the management of the standing organization. At the organizational level this can be enhanced by implementing a project management methodology, based on these good practices.

In a nutshell, this pocket book is intended as a key contributor and tangible asset, when introducing and reinforcing concepts of project, program and portfolio management in your organization for improved communication and cooperation. It supports an organizational-wide implementation of a project management culture, bringing you the benefits of 'the right projects executed right the first time'!

In chapter 3 you will find a more detailed description about the *PMBOK® Guide*, its fundamental definitions and its structure. In chapters 4 to12 we will further detail the areas of project management knowledge and their underlying processes.

1.2 Practical tips for using this pocket guide

On the additional cover page attached to the back cover of this book, all knowledge areas and applicable processes and chapter numbers are listed. On the pages of the pocket guide each chapter is recognizable by the icon representing the applicable knowledge area on the side of the page, enabling you to quickly locate the appropriate topic.

Key terms and definitions are explained in a restricted selection from the Glossary of the *PMBOK® Guide*, in Appendix A.

1.3 Project management and its value

Every organization has its unique culture and faces diverse challenges. Also, organizations start with a different situation and set of problems to be resolved. In order to define the value of project management, we firstly need to define exactly what is meant by project management, as this is a broad concept. Then we can look at the various aspects of project management and show the value associated with each aspect.

> *PMI Definition:*
> Project management is the application of knowledge, skills, tools and techniques to meet project requirements.

This is accomplished by the application of project management processes. Research shows that, with the increasing complexity and faster changing environments that businesses are faced with, projects managed by structural application of good practice-based processes show consistently better performance in areas such as, but not limited to:

- 'Deliver as promised' by realistic expectation-setting through up-front project definition, planning, and estimation;
- Faster delivery through the reuse of common and known project management processes;
- Less 'surprises' during project execution, utilizing proactive project management processes;
- Improved customer satisfaction and less rework by delivering the right product or service, right, the first time.

These opportunities as well as the savings offered by organizational project management excellence are tangible. But the value proposition for project management is much greater and also includes less tangible benefits like:

- A highly committed and motivated team that can work together through effective communication and goal setting;
- An inspiring project environment with a 'can-do' mentality through ambitious yet realistic commitments;
- Transparent and improved decision making at all organizational levels through more effective project communication.

These qualitative benefits will even reinforce the quantitative advantages, which will guarantee that an organization is able to excel.

Several companies have built a good reputation for being able to consistently deliver top quality projects. However, a majority of organizations are still struggling with this. Do you recognize the following characteristics?

- Projects mostly deliver late, over-budget, or without meeting the functionality requirements of the project sponsor and end-users;
- Project managers do it 'their way' as there are no, or poor, standards for project management processes and techniques;
- Project management is regarded as an overhead instead of being recognized as providing business value;
- The project work undertaken by resources from within the line organization is not carefully planned for as part of the operations planning, but is typically regarded as 'next to your primary function';
- Project budgets do not include the cost of internal workforce as they are 'already paid for';
- There is no overall insight available on all the projects being undertaken in the organization, nor their cost versus the added value;
- The required work for managing projects proactively is not included in the project plan;

- Projects may be somehow 'successful' in the end but only through heavy stress and overtime work.

> *Do you recognize the above? Having disciplined project management is the way to overcome these shortcomings. The value of a good project management practice, using standard project management processes, will enable better communication to deal with contingencies pro-actively. This will substantially and continuously increase the chances of project success. It will establish new management procedures and processes. It will enable you to run your organization as an economic enterprise.*

1.4 Successfully fulfilling your role as project sponsor, project team member or project manager

Understanding your role in a project and acting accordingly is vital for project success. Therefore we highlight the three key roles which are the major contributors in realizing a successful project:

1. The **project sponsor** acts as the continuous link between the line organization and the project. It is the sponsor who is responsible at the start for defining the business case for the project; why should we do this project; what are the organization's needs? When the project is approved and the project manager takes over the responsibility for 'delivery of the defined project result', the sponsor still fulfills an ever-important role. The sponsor should, amongst other things, ensure that the organization sticks to its initial decisions, preventing constant priority changes based on daily operational issues. The project sponsor, therefore, plays an important role in ensuring that there is sufficient support from functional and operational management, which in turn fulfills a key role in assigning the appropriate resources to the project

team. The sponsor should also support the organization's readiness to effectively deal with the project result when it is delivered, as this is where the benefits realization will start. The project sponsor must work closely with the project manager. The fluent communication between them is crucial for the project and organizational success.

2. The **project (management) team member** is typically responsible for delivering the expertise and work needed to create the project result. During the initial phases of the project, their focus is on defining the best approach and developing a feasible high-level plan for the project; in other words, the preparation. During the execution they realize the project end-result and specific sub-components, based on their expertise. Sufficient representation within the project team, of the organization which takes over the project result at the end of the project is essential, in order to ensure the smooth transition of the project result to the standing or sponsoring organization.
3. The **project manager** is ultimately responsible for the delivery of the defined project result. Key elements in this role are stakeholder management, and guiding the project team and the appropriate stakeholders in selecting and applying the right project management processes at the right time. But everything must be undertaken with an eye on the delivery of the project result. The project manager must take advantage of the project sponsor's business knowledge and influential position. He/she must escalate to him/her all issues or business- related problems that they are not able to solve themselves.

In every project, these key roles that are needed for the successful delivery of the project, should be clearly described and understood, so that every stakeholder can act accordingly.

Figure 1.1 clearly describes the common relationships between the line and project organization, and shows where each role is positioned.

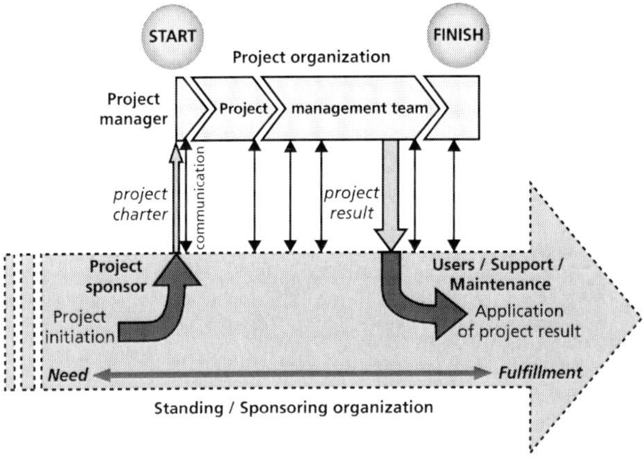

Figure 1.1 Common relationship between line and project organization

1.5 FAQ

We have identified some typical questions one could ask when first confronted with project management or the *PMBOK® Guide*.

What is a project?

> *PMI Definition:*
> A project is a temporary endeavor undertaken to create a unique product, service or result.

This means:

- It has a defined start and end, otherwise it's not temporary;
- It has a certain 'volume' of work which needs some form of organization, otherwise it's not an endeavor;

- It is not business as usual, not following normal procedures, because there is something unique to it;
- It creates an end result, being a product, a service or result.

There are projects of all sorts and levels, demanding that project management activities should be geared to the project at hand. But it remains the organization's responsibility to decide if the desired result should be realized by means of undertaking a project.

Is 'project management' a profession?

While there is no agreed definition of a 'profession', you could describe it as:
'A disciplined group of individuals who adhere to defined ethical standards and uphold themselves to the public as having specific knowledge and skills in a generally recognized, organized body of learning, derived from education and training, and who apply this knowledge and these skills in the interest of others.'

With projects getting more and more complex, the demands on a project manager's competence are also increasing. For example, everyone can apply a bandage to a wound but that does not make everyone a doctor. The need to obtain specific skills, knowledge and education, in order to successfully fulfill the role of project manager, is generally recognized. This is even confirmed in the Academic world where Masters degrees in Project Management are now available.

Typically for professions like lawyers, doctors, etc. the responsibility for the welfare, health and safety of the community takes precedence over other considerations. This aspect is also confirmed by PMI's 'Code of Ethics', the signing of which is an eligibility requirement for obtaining a PMI credential. One can therefore conclude that 'project management has become a profession.

Can you manage a line organization effectively without projects?

Line organizations are typically function-centric and, in general, focus on 'doing their thing better', and are therefore mostly resistant to changes outside their function. Projects and project management are all about realizing changes. No organization can survive in today's environment without having projects. At times they are not formally recognized but organizations undertake them anyway. The increasing number of 'reorganizations' reflect this, with a constant drive for ensuring the line organization keeps up with the increasingly complex and ever-faster changes in the environment. The increasing number and level of changes, as well as the risks associated to these, are demanding greater focus and attention on projects, together with the need for a more professional approach towards project management. This ensures that the changes are delivered and managed in an appropriate way. It will support line organizations in continuing to 'do the right thing, the best way'.

What is the purpose of the *PMBOK® Guide*?

The *PMBOK® Guide* describes a professional approach towards project management, which is applicable to most projects. This approach is based on its proven value and benefits in practice, through the contribution of thousands of project managers worldwide.

Is the *PMBOK® Guide* a methodology?

The *PMBOK® Guide* is referred to as a framework. A framework can be defined as a basic conceptual structure to allow homogenous handling of different business processes grouped together, i.e. business units. It also increases management discipline. It pre-defines common deliverables to and from each business process. A framework is a well-defined tactic to master the complex environment of an organization in a simple fashion. It acts as a taxonomy or map of the entire body of project management knowledge.

A methodology can be defined as a system of methods that are followed in a particular discipline. A method describes the process by which a task is completed; a prescribed way to execute the processes. Being a basic reference the *PMBOK® Guide* is more of a framework than a methodology. Although the project management processes are described, together with the tools and techniques commonly applied, it does not prescribe the exact way of doing. In practice, for the implementation of this framework, several project management methodologies can be defined and applied, fine-tuned towards the application area and specific subject of the projects. But before one can select, define, or apply any project management methodology, there should first be a thorough and common understanding of the project management framework.

How is this pocket edition aligned with the *PMBOK® Guide* and what if you want to know more?

Creating a shared view, a common structure, and then consistently building on that, is essential for clear and concise communication. For this reason we have simply maintained the well-considered structure of the *PMBOK® Guide*. Therefore chapters 1 to 3 form a high-level introduction for building this common view, just as the first three chapters of the *PMBOK® Guide* do in a much more detailed level. We have then ensured full alignment of this pocket guide with the original *PMBOK® Guide* in the numbering of Chapters 4 to 12 as well as their sub paragraphs (e.g. 4.1. Develop Project Charter). So, when looking for a more detailed explanation and understanding about a certain subject, simply refer to the related chapter and paragraph number in the *PMBOK® Guide*.

Can you get certified on the *PMBOK® Guide* as an individual or as an organization?

PMI set up several individual certifications, for the typical project manager roles, of which the Certified Associate in Project Management (CAPM)® and the Project Management Professional (PMP)® use the *PMBOK® Guide* as a basis. PMI does not issue organizational certifications in the same way that ISO or ANSI do.

How can the *PMBOK® Guide* support you in real-life application?

As the *PMBOK® Guide* is based on good practices, it can effectively act as a 'worldwide lessons learned database'. Based on its structure and well defined processes, it will definitely turn the mind-set from an 'ad-hoc' and fire-fighting mode, towards a more proactively oriented approach. It enables you, when faced with challenging project situations, to quickly refer to the appropriate project management process, and fine-tune these to your project. It directly enhances the project communications by creating a common understanding of 'projects' and a shared vision on how to manage these the best way.

How does the *PMBOK® Guide* align with other standards, frameworks and methodologies?

The *PMBOK® Guide* provides a framework that is generally accepted as global good practice for project management. Therefore it is a perfect guideline for creating and understanding your organizational project management methodology, which needs to fit with your specific projects in your specific environment. This is typically where the project management processes and the content creation processes should be integrated. 'Drowning' people in several different methodologies, with different backgrounds and definitions, and having each individual doing their own 'integration exercise', is likely to cause confusion, errors and miscommunication, as well as being inefficient. A well-organized comparison of the processes, terms and definitions of the *PMBOK® Guide* with the processes, terms and definitions of other standards, frameworks and methodologies applied in your organization, will enable a quick identification of any potential overlap, and enable effective integration in an appropriate way.

How does the *PMBOK® Guide* address the different organizational entities and levels?

Organizations develop procedures for delivering results in a predictable way that allow them to manage expectations. However, as most projects are cross-functional, several organizational entities typically come together in projects and are required to deal with situations not encountered before, and for which no procedures are defined (as yet). As projects result in changes in organizations, the appropriate stakeholders are involved, leading to the involvement of different organizational levels, i.e. operations level, tactical level, and even strategic level. Therefore the understanding and application of a common organizational-wide reference such as the *PMBOK® Guide* is of particular value in such situations.

Is the *PMBOK® Guide* likely to supersede our current (organizationally developed) project management approach or methodology?

Organizationally-developed project management approaches or methodologies mostly stem from a recognized need for improvement in project management application, based on organizational experiences and good practices. As the *PMBOK® Guide* is also based on good practices, the majority of your own project management methodology will not drastically change. However, maintaining these good practices, as well as ensuring continuous alignment with latest developments in the project management profession, can become very costly and time consuming. This is the major reason why organizations switch to simply taking the *PMBOK® Guide* as their basic reference for a project management standard and only adjust this where appropriate, documenting this transparently. Following the Pareto rule; around 80% of the standard is likely to be generally applicable to your type of projects. This allows a focus on the specific 20% of the project management processes which form the uniqueness of your organization. This becomes the heart of your project management methodology.

Most generic project management methodologies, publicly available, refer to the *PMBOK® Guide* as a basic framework. In such cases the knowledge contained in the *PMBOK® Guide* substantially supports the better understanding and positioning of this project management methodology, thus reinforcing the right application.

What if I need more information?

As this is a pocket book, it should be considered as introductory summary of the *PMBOK® Guide* and PMI. Far more details and explanations on certain subjects can be found in the *PMBOK® Guide*. Also PMI's website, **www.pmi.org**, will give you access to more detailed information.

Chapter 2
The organization behind the *PMBOK® Guide* – The Project Management Institute (PMI)

2.1 PMI's facts and figures

PMI is a worldwide not-for-profit Professional Association for advancing the practice, science and profession of project management throughout the world.

With project management being a relatively young profession, the official announcement of PMI's founding came on October 9, 1969 during a project management seminar in Atlanta, Georgia (USA). It was recognized that there were many management practices shared in different types of projects. From then it developed to the largest project management organization worldwide, based on the commitment of volunteers who were passionate about developing and supporting the profession of project management. Crucial in this development has been a publication in the Project Management Journal in 1983. There the first 'Standards baseline for project management' – being the predecessor of the current *PMBOK® Guide* – next to a Code of Ethics for project management professionals and guidelines for accreditation and certification were issued. The long-term growth of PMI membership has been remarkably steady, averaging close to 20% per year; 1,000 members in 1975, 10,000 in 1994, 100,000 in 2003, with numbers growing towards 400,000 in 2012. PMI and its initiatives are primarily run by volunteers, apart from a relatively small professional organization for managing such an extensive membership association. 'For its members and by its members' is a major PMI managing principle.

2.2 Available global standards of PMI

One of the continuous and highly recognized initiatives of PMI is the development of global standards. A standard provides guidelines, rules and characteristics for the topic it is covering. Global standards are crucial to the project management profession. They ensure that a basic project management framework is applied consistently worldwide, which reinforces a common 'language' and approach and simplifies communication between stakeholders. This is especially important when managing international and cross-organizational initiatives, where different stakeholders have different backgrounds.

The currently available PMI standards are broken down into three categories:

- Foundational Standards;
- Practice Standards and Frameworks;
- Standards Extensions.

Foundational Standards

These standards provide a shared foundation for project management and represent the four key areas of the profession: project, program, portfolio and the organizational approach to project management.

- A Guide to the Project Management Body of Knowledge (*PMBOK® Guide*), including translations into 10 different languages;
- The Standard for Program Management;
- The Standard for Portfolio Management;
- Organizational Project Management Maturity Model (OPM3®).

Practice Standards and Frameworks

Practice standards are guides to a tool, technique or process identified in the *PMBOK® Guide* or other standards.

- Practice Standard for Project Risk Management;
- Practice Standard for Earned Value Management;
- Practice Standard for Project Configuration Management;
- Practice Standard for Work Breakdown Structures;
- Practice Standard for Scheduling;
- Practice Standard for Project Estimating;
- Project Manager Competency Development Framework.

PMI Standards Extensions

Standard extensions expand upon standards for specific project types or industries.

- Construction Extension to the *PMBOK® Guide*;
- Government Extension to the *PMBOK® Guide*.

PMI's standards are continuously maintained and updated to incorporate the latest developments and insights in the profession, while new standards are also under development. A high level of consistency has been achieved between all these standards, especially regarding terminology and definitions, which reinforces the application of a common language.

In general, personalized digital copies are available to PMI members free of charge!

2.3 Available certifications

Certification is valued by both individuals and organizations for the development, and assessment of compliance with professional project management standards. Recognizing this, PMI administers a globally recognized professional certification program that promotes the development of the project management profession. It supports business professionals in commencing, building or advancing their careers in project, program and portfolio management. It provides organizations with a good reference for assessing the expected knowledge and experience level of individuals labeling themselves as 'project managers', as this is not a restricted term. It also supports HR managers in setting up career paths in the area of project management.

Currently PMI offers the following credentials, reflecting different levels and areas of experience:

- Certified Associate in Project Management (CAPM)®;
- Project Management Professional (PMP)®;
- PMI Agile Certified Practitioner (PMI-ACP[2])®;
- Program Management Professional (PgMP)®;
- PMI Risk Management Professional (PMI-RMP)SM;
- PMI Scheduling Professional (PMI-SP)SM.

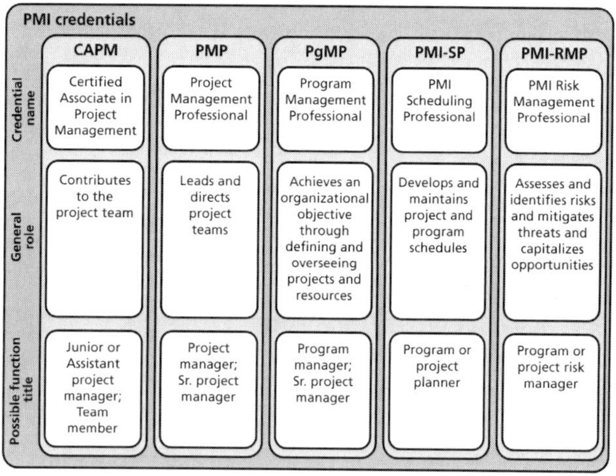

Figure 2.1 PMI credentials (source: PMI Inc.)

Code of Ethics

As a typical characteristic of 'professions', PMI issued the *Code of Ethics and Professional Conduct* which applies globally. When dealing with any stakeholder, practitioners should be committed to honest and fair practices and respectful dealings. Certified project managers have explicitly accepted this code of ethics, as it is a requirement for certification by PMI.

2.4 Geographical representation of PMI and translations

Local chapters

Next to the global organization, most PMI members also join a local chapter, which connects them with a local network of professional expertise. The members receive support and opportunities to meet with peers from various industries through meetings, activities and educational programs. There are currently more than 250 chapters supported by PMI, active in more than 70 countries worldwide.

Other local representation

For effective and simplified communication with its members and other stakeholders, PMI has set up Customer Care, Regional Service Centers, Representative Offices and Relationship Offices around the globe for Asia Pacific, India and Europe-Middle East-Africa (EMEA).

Translations

Being PMI's most important standard, the *PMBOK® Guide*, is officially available in 10 different languages in addition to English:

- Arabic;
- Brazilian Portuguese;
- (Simplified) Chinese;
- French;
- German;
- Italian;
- Japanese;
- Korean;
- Russian;
- Spanish.

Although all examinations for certification are administered in English, language aids are available for these languages, as well as Hebrew and traditional Chinese. In addition to this some local chapters took the initiative of creating their local translations of the *PMBOK® Guide*. These 'unofficial' translations are, however, not supported for examination, unless the local chapter also makes arrangements for that separately.

2.5 Other PMI initiatives

Research program and publications

PMI has a dedicated research arm, responsible for initiating, funding, guiding and coordinating academic research around the world. PMI has already invested over US $16 million in project management research, leading to the release of more than 350 publications. PMI also organizes the PMI Biennial Research and Education Conference bringing together academics and senior practitioners committed to the advancement of empirically-based knowledge in the field.

PMI publications devoted to advancing the discipline of project management include:

- PMI's Project Management Journal®, a quarterly peer-refereed leading academic and research journal;
- PM Network®, an award-winning monthly magazine that covers trends, tools, techniques and good practices;
- PMI Today®, a monthly newsletter delivered with PM Network that keeps members up-to-date on Institute news and events;
- Several online e-newsletters with information targeted to specific audiences, helping readers to remain up-to-date on the news they need.

Communities of Practice

Communities of Practice are interactive places where members with common interests or industries share ideas, challenges and concerns across geographical boundaries. Through networking, developing technical papers, teleconferences and collaborative work on special projects, members grow their knowledge. Examples of Communities of Practice are Aerospace and Defense, Healthcare Information Systems, Project Management Quality, or Project Risk Management.

Registered Education Provider (R.E.P.) network

PMI also supports a so-called Registered Education Provider (R.E.P.) network. This consists of training organizations, and executive development centers at universities, and in companies, that provide high quality project management training services. Their educational offerings have been assessed by PMI. During this assessment, R.E.P. organizations have demonstrated their capability to provide effective project management training.

PMI Registered Consultant Program

The PMI Registered Consultant Program helps organizations find capable consulting firms to assist with implementing project, program or portfolio management aligned to their unique organizational needs as well as to PMI's best practices.

Academic Program Accreditation

The PMI Global Accreditation Center for Project Management (GAC) is the world's leading global accrediting body for project management degree programs. The GAC's mission is to advance excellence in project management education, worldwide, and to ensure that GAC accredited programs meet current and anticipated talent needs for qualified project professionals. Currently over 50 degree programs at more than 20 academic institutions worldwide are accredited by PMI GAC, with several other programs at various stages of the accreditation process.

For more information about PMI, please visit the website at **www.PMI.org.**

Chapter 3
The *PMBOK® Guide* at a glance

In this chapter we will initially focus on the background and the general content of the *PMBOK® Guide*. This will enable you to understand the structure of the publication. Secondly we will cover some concepts from the *PMBOK® Guide* which are regarded as essential knowledge when involved in project environments.

3.1 History of the *PMBOK® Guide*

In 1981 the PMI Board of Directors approved a project of which one area of focus was the development of a project management standard, describing the content and structure of the project management body of knowledge. This project resulted in 1983 in a publication of the project management standards baseline. Being the first publication of its kind, it formed the basis for further discussing and better defining 'Project Management' as a profession. In 1987 a follow-on project resulted in publication of 'The Project Management Body of Knowledge'. Further developments and continued feedback, based upon practical application, resulted in an update in 1996 called 'A Guide to the Project Management Body of Knowledge (*PMBOK® Guide*)'. In 2000 and 2004 the 2nd and 3rd editions respectively were published, reflecting the growth of the knowledge and practices in project management, as well as providing greater clarification. This was finally superseded by the latest update in 2008, the 4th edition. Briefly, the current edition contains over 25 years of practical experience in project management brought together by thousands of practitioners in the field and academics thoroughly investigating the subject of project management.

3.2 Structure of the *PMBOK® Guide*

The *PMBOK® Guide* is structured in three sections. Once you understand this structure, the *PMBOK® Guide* provides an excellent framework for supporting the professional management of projects.

- Section 1, (Chapters 1 and 2) called 'The Project Management Framework', discusses the purpose of the *PMBOK® Guide*, as well as giving a brief introduction to the key concepts of project management by covering topics such as:
  - Definition of a project;
  - What is project management;
  - Relationships among project, program and portfolio management;
  - The difference between project management and operations management;
  - The role of the project manager;
  - How the project environment can enhance or constrain the project management options;
  - The project lifecycle;
  - Stakeholders;
  - Organizational concepts.
- Section 2, (Chapter 3) called 'The Standard for Project Management of a Project' defines and describes the **42 project management processes** that are recognized as good practice, and thus applicable to most projects. These project management processes are grouped together and discussed as such in the following **five project management process groups**:
  - Initiating;
  - Planning;
  - Executing;
  - Monitoring and controlling;
  - Closing.

These are further explained in paragraph 3.8 of this pocket book.

- Section 3 (Chapter 4-12) further elaborates on these defined project management processes. In order to do so, the *PMBOK® Guide* identifies **nine Project Management Knowledge Areas**, these being specific areas of required knowledge for managing a project. For each Knowledge Area the applicable project management processes are discussed in more detail, using a structure describing:
  - The process input;
  - The tools and techniques which can be applied for performing the process;
  - The process output.

Inputs and outputs are documents or documentable items. An output from one process is quite often an input for another process.

3.3 Project – program – portfolio

In practice the above terms are quite often mixed up or applied rather loosely, causing a lot of misunderstanding and miscommunication, including unclear roles and responsibilities. The *PMBOK® Guide* supplies following definitions for project, program and portfolio management as well as providing a comparative overview.

PMI definitions:

Project: A temporary endeavor undertaken to create a unique product, service or result.

Program: A group of related projects managed in a coordinated way to obtain benefits and control not available from managing them individually. Programs may include elements of related work outside of the scope of the discrete projects in the program.

Portfolio: A collection of projects and programs and other work that are grouped together to facilitate effective management of that work to meet strategic business objectives. The projects or programs of the portfolio may not necessarily be interdependent or directly related.

Below a comparative overview of project, program and portfolio management is given.

	PROJECTS	PROGRAMS	PORTFOLIOS
Scope	Projects have defined objectives. Scope is progressively elaborated throughout the project life cycle.	Programs have a larger scope and provide more significant benefits.	Portfolios have a business scope that changes with the strategic goals of the organization.
Change	Project managers expect change and implement processes to keep change managed and controlled.	The program managers must expect change from both inside and outside the program and be prepared to manage it.	Portfolio managers continually monitor changes in the broad environment.
Planning	Project managers progressively elaborate high-level information into detailed plans throughout the project life cycle.	Program managers develop the overall program plan and create high-level plans to guide detailed planning at the component level.	Portfolio managers create and maintain necessary processes and communication relative to the aggregate portfolio.
Management	Project managers manage the project team to meet the project objectives.	Program managers manage the program staff and the project managers; they provide vision and overall leadership.	Portfolio managers may manage or coordinate portfolio management staff.

	PROJECTS	PROGRAMS	PORTFOLIOS
Success	Success is measured by product and project quality, timelines, budget compliance, and degree of customer satisfaction.	Success is measured by the degree of which the program satisfies the needs and benefits for which is was undertaken.	Success is measured in terms of aggregate performance of portfolio components.
Monitoring	Project managers monitor and control the work of producing the products, services or results that the project was undertaken to produce.	Program managers monitor the progress of program components to ensure the overall goals, schedules, budget, and benefits of the program will be met.	Portfolio managers monitor aggregate performance and value indicators.

Figure 3.1 Comparative overview of project, program and portfolio management

PMI issues the *PMBOK® Guide* for project management, focusing on 'doing the projects the right way'. PMI also issues seperate standards for program and portfolio management, focusing on 'doing the right projects'.

3.4 Project lifecycle

PMI definition: A project lifecycle is a collection of generally sequential project phases whose name and number are determined by the control needs of the organization or organizations involved in the project, the nature of the project itself, and its area of application.

A project lifecycle consists of project phases, generally sequential. What it looks like - the names and number of phases - is entirely defined by the organizations involved in the project. Not too much detail, nor too high level, and well aligned to the project application area. As it is the primary reference for organizing the communication around the project, the project lifecycle should be understandable to all stakeholders involved. It provides a valuable means of communicating to senior management about the high-level project approach and progress, as well as for communicating at a more detailed level, in order to properly position these details in relation to the 'big picture'.

A project lifecycle can be further explained in detail and supported in practical application with a methodology. Some application areas like IT or the Construction sector have project lifecycle structures with common phase names which are well documented and applied throughout the respective sector, e.g. 'define – design – build – test – implement'.

Insufficient integration of project management processes and product creation oriented processes in a project lifecycle cause projects to fail. Many application area-based lifecycles are very product or 'content' oriented, typically lacking sufficient focus on the right organizational scope and set-up during the project start-up, as well as insufficient attention from the outset on a well defined hand-over and transitioning. They also frequently fail to ensure proper maintenance and support after the project life, which is required to enable a proper project close down.

Typically a project lifecycle is contained within one or more product lifecycles, or when the project objective is not a product, the lifecycle of the service or of any other result.

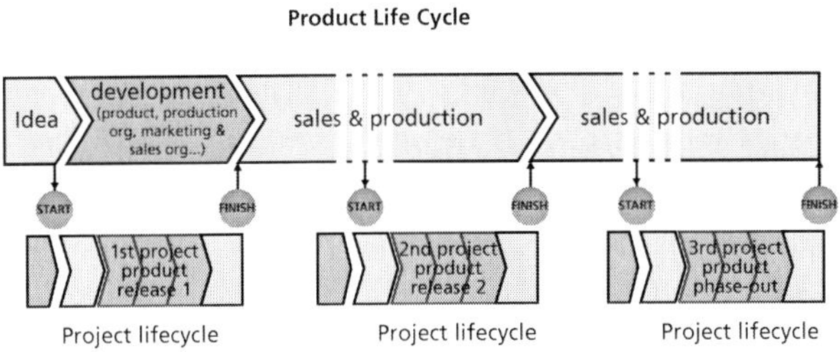

Figure 3.2 Project lifecycle as part of a product lifecycle (Based on source: PMI Inc.)

In general project lifecycles can have the following structures:

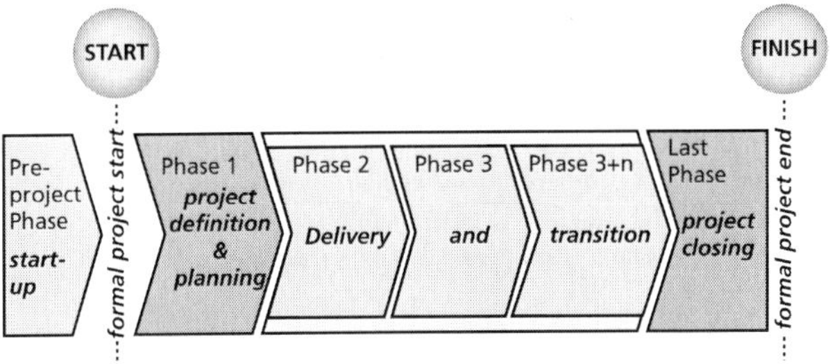

Figure 3.3 Example of a project lifecycle (PLC) (Based on source: PMI Inc.)

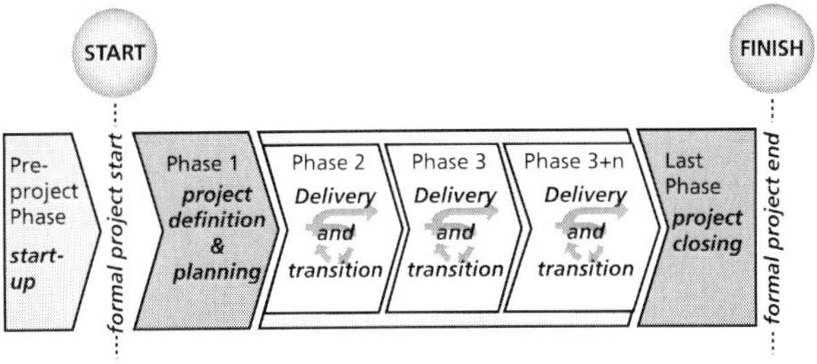

Figure 3.4 Example of a PLC with cyclic approach

3.5 Project phases

Project phases are divisions within a project where extra control is needed to effectively manage the completion of a deliverable. Project phases are mostly sequential but may overlap in specific project situations. The phases are part of the project lifecycle.

A very simple project may have only one phase, but in such a case one could, of course, reconsider the need for approaching the work as a project. Is it really an 'endeavor' which justifies the formal set up of a separate temporary organizational structure? Or is it just 'a more than average complex task' which needs a bit more management attention and communication?

Large projects can have several phases. Again, it is the responsibility of the project manager and the project management team to break down the project into manageable pieces.

3.6 Project management process groups

The project management processes are grouped together in five project management process groups:

- Initiating process group, for defining a new project or (sub)phase and obtaining authorization to start;
- Planning process group - for establishing the plan of the project or detailed plan per (sub)phase;
- Executing process group - for executing the plan and completing the work, thus creating the planned deliverables of the project or (sub) phase;
- Monitoring and controlling process group - for tracking and reviewing the project work, project performance management, and the proper identification and management of changes;
- Closing process group - for formally closing a phase or the project.

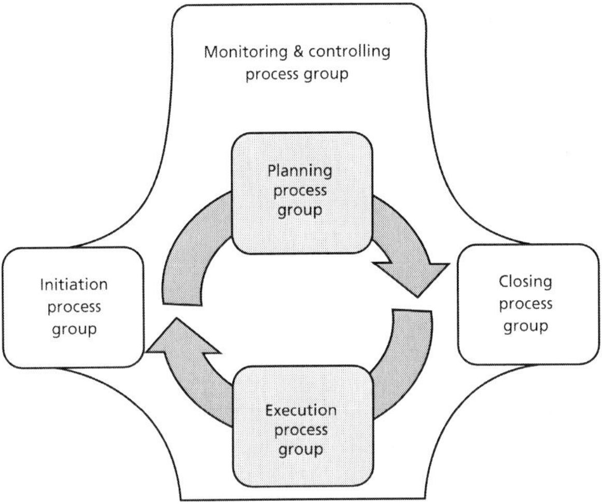

Figure 3.5 Process groups (source: PMI)

These process groups are required for every project and performed in a logical sequence. **Process groups are not the same as the project phases**, as process groups are often iterated in a project. Normally process groups are executed at a high-level first, for the whole project, and repeated at the level of every project phase, sub-phase or even work package.

The process groups are guides for applying proper project management. It enables the quick identification of the focus point of a given project, at a given time during the project life cycle, and subsequently triggering the applicable project management processes.

Also the process groups are repeated in each phase but on a more detailed level.

Important: *project phases are not the same as project management process groups!*

Although sometimes these look more or less the same, the project management process groups focus on the project management oriented deliverables. But most of all we need to recognize the project's product-oriented processes, as these create the end result of the project, and that's what the project is all about of course! In the phases we therefore recognize a mix of project management processes and activities, and the primary project product-oriented processes and activities.

3.7 Stakeholders

PMI Definition: Stakeholders are persons or organizations who are actively involved in the project, or whose interests may be positively or negatively affected by the performance or completion of the project.

Identifying and understanding the project's stakeholders is crucial in enabling the project manager and the team to do the right thing and communicate appropriately, and thus manage expectations. The stakeholders define the project's requirements. Stakeholders will also try to influence the project depending on their position and their own interests.

Stakeholders are usually grouped together as follows:

- Internal to the project;
- External to project but internal to the performing organization;
- External to the project and to performing organization.

The exact positioning of the stakeholders (internal or external to the performing organization) may differ from project to project.

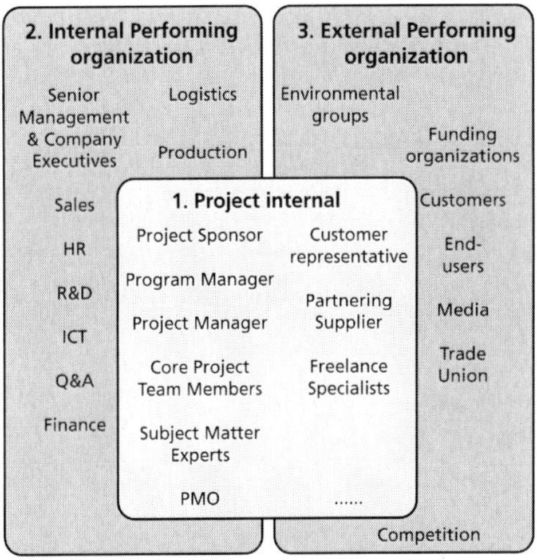

Figure 3.6 Stakeholders overview

The project manager, the project team members and the project sponsor are the most important stakeholders and their mutual consultations form the basis of effective communication towards other stakeholders.

3.8 Organizational structure

The structure of the sponsoring organization is an important environmental factor in a project as it influences how different project stakeholders will behave, based on their interest and organizational position, how project resources are obtained and assigned, and how the project itself is organized. We distinguish the following different structures, together with their main characteristics.

Functional organization

This is the 'classic' organization where staff are grouped by specialty (production, marketing, sales, etc.). The advantage of this organizational form is that it allows for improved knowledge and skills development in each area, thus 'doing the specific job better, faster, cheaper'. The formal power resides with the functional managers as staff report to them. Projects are coordinated between the functional managers. Every department performs its part of the project independently. There remains a strong 'silo' oriented attitude, which is not the best supporting approach when there is a need to work together for a 'common' cause.

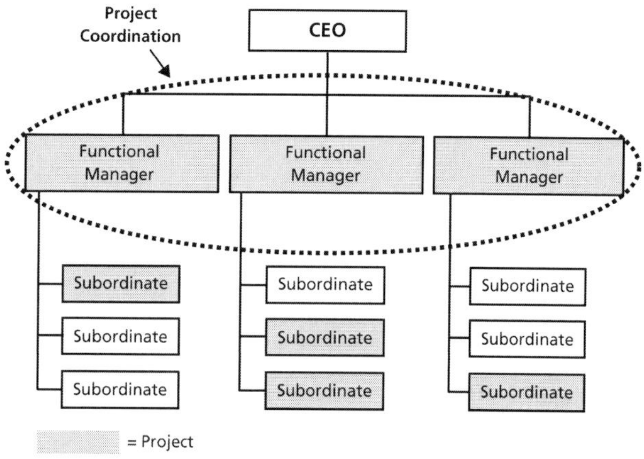

Figure 3.7 Functional organization

Projectized organization

Typically the majority of the resources are involved in project work, generally full-time assigned to one project. The staff is, therefore, grouped per project and they report to a project manager. The project managers all have the same authority, comparable to the authority that functional managers have in the functional organization. The knowledge and skills development of specialists may, however, suffer due to this highly project-centric approach.

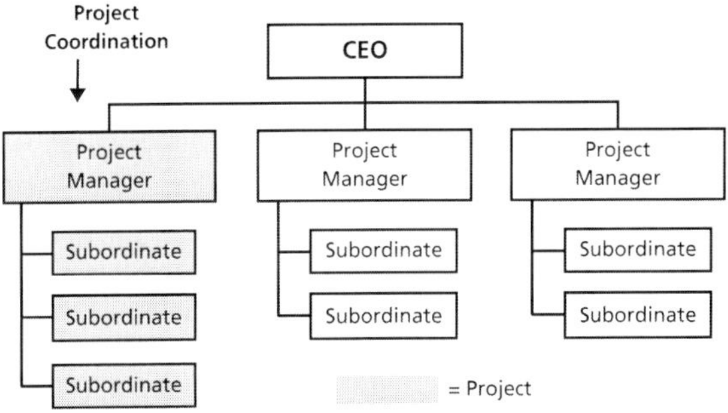

Figure 3.8 Projectized organization

Matrix organizations

This type of organization is a blend of the functional and the projectized organization. There are typically three different variants - weak matrix, balanced matrix and strong matrix.

A **balanced matrix** organization recognizes the need of a project manager and they are usually assigned full-time. Other project resources however remain fully under the responsibility of the functional departments. Clear communication and decision making is essential between functional managers and project managers about roles and responsibilities and authority, as this becomes one of the key issues if it is not properly arranged. 'Project managers' reside in a functional department. Acquiring the appropriate resources is the challenge. The staff's priority is mostly with their prime function-related tasks as this is what their performance is evaluated upon. Acquiring the necessary resources from other departments is an even bigger challenge as it is not seen as 'their project'. As a result, projects generally experience major challenges around resource availability when proper program and portfolio management is lacking.

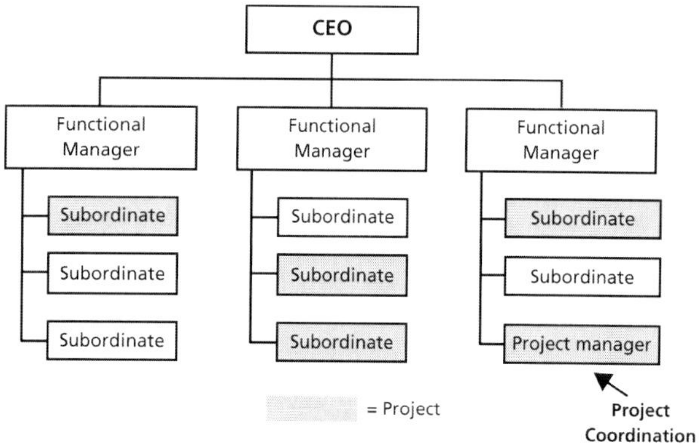

Figure 3.9 Balanced matrix

In a **weak matrix** the characteristics of the functional organization are still predominant. Here the project manager has more of a coordinating role, rather than really leading the project, and it is regarded as a part-time and secondary role.

In a **strong matrix** the characteristics of the projectized organization prevail. The project manager is regarded as a full-time function and the project managers are grouped together in one functional 'project management' unit. Other project resources, however, still reside in other functional departments.

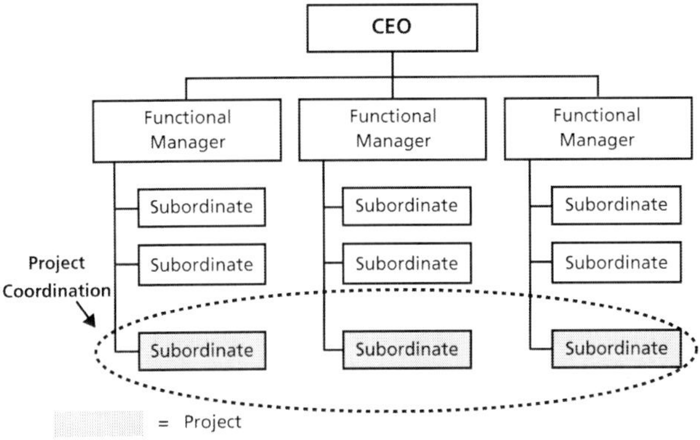

Figure 3.10 Weak matrix

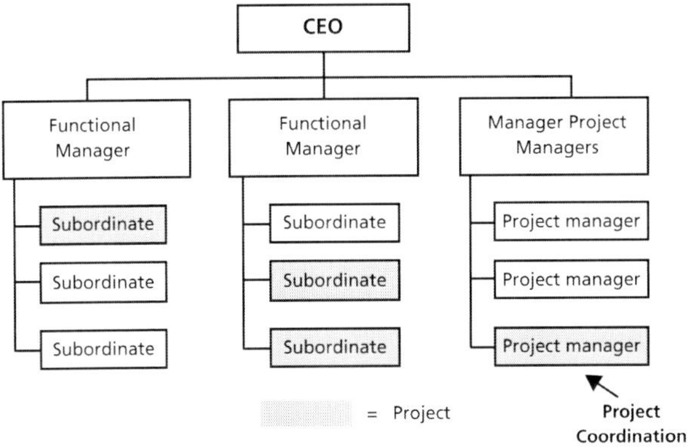

Figure 3.11 Strong matrix

The composite structure

In practice, many organizations, although essentially being functionally organized, create additional structures for specific projects at hand. Typically for business-critical projects, realizing large organizational changes, a projectized structure is set up. For example, this may entail having a project manager reporting directly to the CEO, with dedicated project resources reporting to the project manager, specific administrative support and project operating procedures, often by-passing or overruling enterprise procedures.

It is also worth noting that projectized organizations can set up functional structures for those project components that have a high recurring character and sufficient volume. In this way the efficiency and knowledge sharing for these components is improved.

3.9 Project management knowledge areas

PMI recognizes nine so-called knowledge areas, numbered 4 to12 according to their chapters in the *PMBOK® Guide*. The areas are defined by their specific knowledge requirements that a project manager should be familiar with in order to do a professional job. These identified areas of project management are described in terms of processes, practices, inputs, outputs, and tools and techniques. These knowledge areas are described in more detail in chapters 4 to 12, as follows:

- Chapter 4 - Project Integration Management;
- Chapter 5 - Project Scope Management;
- Chapter 6 - Project Time Management;
- Chapter 7 - Project Cost Management;
- Chapter 8 - Project Quality Management;
- Chapter 9 - Project Human Resource Management;
- Chapter 10 - Project Communications Management;

- Chapter 11 - Project Risk Management;
- Chapter 12 - Project Procurement Management.

3.10 Project management processes

PMI identifies 42 project management processes which are, in general, applicable to most projects. These processes are structured in the five project management process groups (see section 3.6), and in the respective nine knowledge areas (see section 3.9). This is shown in the additional cover page which can be used as a constant reference when reading this pocket guide.

Chapter 4
Project Integration Management

Project Integration Management is about planning the work and working the plan. It covers the start and finish of the project and everything in between. It is about finding balances between competing objectives, finding alternatives and handling the dependencies between the various project management knowledge areas.

Project Integration Management coordinates the processes from the other knowledge areas.

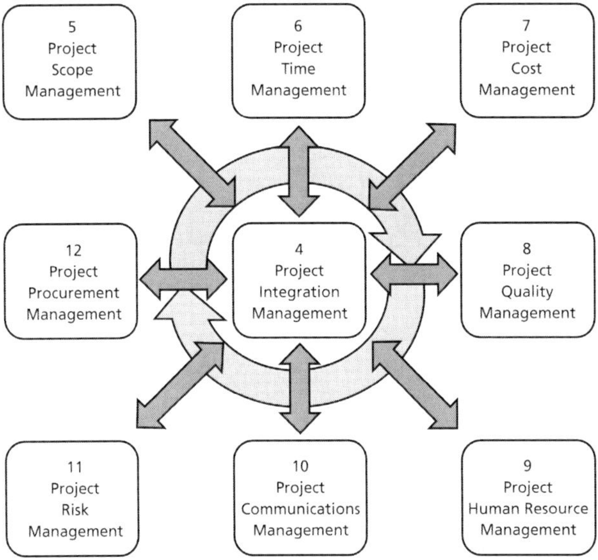

Figure 4.1 The process scheme of Project Integration Management

The Project Integration Management processes are:

1. Develop Project Charter: the process to document the high level requirements and project boundaries - the charter will authorize the project manager to start the project or phase;
2. Develop Project Management Plan: compiling the overall plan by capturing the subsidiary plans that originate from the other eight knowledge areas: 'planning the work';
3. Direct and Manage Project Execution: 'working the plan';
4. Monitor and Control Project Work: this is managing the project's progress;
5. Perform Integrated Change Control: managing the changes to the plan and to the deliverables;
6. Close Project or Phase: completing all activities to close the project or phase.

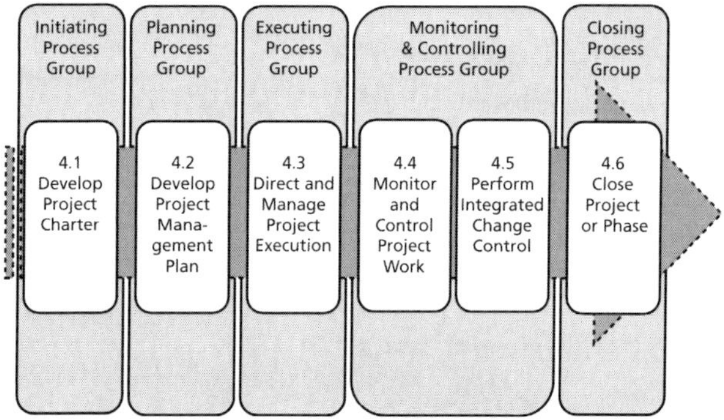

Figure 4.2 Overview of sections in Chapter 4 with Project Integration Management processes

Every Project Manager must pay special attention to change requests within the project. All of the monitoring and control processes and many of the executing processes in the *PMBOK® Guide* may produce change requests as outputs.

In Project Integration Management processes, change requests may follow the route as described in figure 4.3.

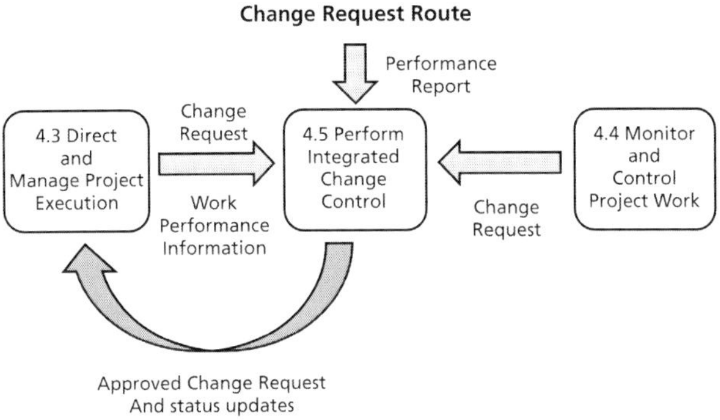

Figure 4.3 Change request route

Both 'Direct and Manage Project Execution' and 'Monitor and Control Project Work' may issue change requests. These requests are assessed and approved, or rejected by 'Perform Integrated Change Control'. All approved change requests are fed back into 'Direct and Manage Project Execution' for implementation. This process will provide work performance information that is used by 'Perform Integrated Change Control' to update the status of the change request in the change request log.

4.1 Develop Project Charter

Develop Project Charter is the process to create the document that will formally mark the start of the project. It describes the envisaged project in terms of the:

- Raison d'être;
- Objectives and success criteria;
- Requirements;
- Risks;
- Timeline and milestones;
- Budget;
- Governance (authority levels);
- Stakeholders;
- Project manager.

The Project Charter should provide a high-level answer to the ' why, what, how, who, when, where' questions.

It is strongly recommended to appoint a project manager as early as possible so he/she can contribute to the compilation of the Project Charter.

Approval of the Project Charter by the requesting organization authorizes the project manager to apply resources to the project activities. The requesting organization is usually represented by a sponsor, the PMO, program manager, portfolio manager or a funding steering committee.

Projects are usually triggered by a certain internal or external business need translated into a so-called business case. A business case will not only provide the business justification in terms of the expected return on investment but will also clarify why the project result is needed (commercial, technical, social, legal or ecological reasons). The business case also must link the envisaged project to the existing strategic goals of the business.

The business case is therefore an essential input to the Project Charter.

In cases where the project is to be undertaken for a customer, the contract should be aligned with the Project Charter.

4.2 Develop Project Management Plan

The Project Management Plan is 'the plan of plans'. It integrates all the baselines and subsidiary management plans from the other eight knowledge areas:

- Schedule baseline (see Chapter 6);
- Cost performance baseline (see Chapter 7);
- Scope baseline (see Chapter 5);
- Scope management plan (see Chapter 5);
- Requirements management plan (see Chapter 5);
- Schedule management plan (see Chapter 6);
- Cost management plan (see Chapter 7);
- Quality management plan (see Chapter 8);
- Process improvement plan (see Chapter 8);
- Human resource plan (see Chapter 9);
- Communications management plan (see Chapter 10);
- Risk management plan (see Chapter 11);
- Procurement management plan (see Chapter 12).

The three aforementioned baselines (the first three bullet points) can also be combined into a Performance Measurement Baseline used for Earned Value measurements (see Chapter 7).

The Project Management Plan will also include a Change Management Plan that describes how changes will be controlled, together with a Configuration Management Plan that describes how configuration items will be managed. It will also address how open issues will be handled.

It is important to ensure that the Project Management Plan fits its purpose. It should be tailored in such a way that it documents how the project work will be executed, in terms of:

- What lifecycle will the project run through?
- What exact project processes will be applied to each phase?
- What tools and techniques will be used to meet the requirements?

The Project Management Plan is not a one-off product, it might well require updates throughout the project lifecycle triggered by the actual work performance results.

4.3 Direct and Manage Project Execution

Where the Project Charter and the Project Management Plan address the 'plan the work' part of the project, Direct and Manage Project Execution is all about 'working the plan'. This focuses upon accomplishing the project requirements, building the deliverables and managing the project team members. It is also about resource allocation, establishing the communication channels and facilitating project forecasting by generating project progress data (time, cost and quality). In addition it covers change, risk and supplier management.

It is in this process that the bare essence of the project materializes: it results in deliverables: 'any unique and verifiable product, result or capability to perform a service that must be produced to complete a process, phase or project' as defined by the *PMBOK® Guide*.

Next to the deliverables, this process also provides the work performance information in terms of deliverable status, schedule progress and costs incurred.

In case issues are encountered during the performance of the work, change requests are issued which may impact upon the scope, cost, schedule and/or quality of the project. These change requests can include corrective or preventive actions, defect repair recommendations or updates to formally controlled documents or plans.

4.4 Monitor and Control Project Work

Monitor and Control Project Work covers the management of a project's progress to ensure that performance objectives are being met. Monitoring is performed throughout the project according to the *PMBOK® Guide*: 'Continuous monitoring gives the project management team insight into the health of the project, and identifies any areas that may require special attention.'

Controlling Project Work includes establishing corrective or preventive actions and following up on action plans to check if these actions have resolved the performance issue.

The project management team uses the project performance reports (see Chapter 10), to compare actual project performance against the Project Management Plan. The outcome of the assessment can lead to the recommendation of corrective or preventive actions and to the identification of new risks.

4.5 Perform Integrated Change Control

Perform Integrated Change Control is the process of managing change in the project context. It is about reviewing and subsequently approving or rejecting change requests and, as a consequence, managing the changes to deliverables, project management documents and project management plan elements.

Since uncontrolled extension of the scope (aka scope creep) is a common risk for all projects, strict change request management is key to keeping the project under control. 'Change' is a fact of life and projects without change do not exist; hence the need for Integrated Change Control.

Only approved changes are allowed to be implemented. The review of the change request and its documented impact analysis is the basis for sound decision making. The implementation of changes requires strict coordination in order to control their impact across the project. A change to the project requirements can affect schedule, cost, risk, quality and staffing.

A tool that can be used to assist in this process is a configuration management system with integrated change control. It will provide a professional way to centrally manage the changes and the baselines. Change control covers the identification, documentation and control of the changes within the project.

The process of performing Integrated Change Control can be streamlined by establishing a Change Control Board (CCB) that meets frequently to asses, document and decide on change requests. Appropriate stakeholders must have a say in who the members of the CCB will be and what their exact roles and responsibilities are.

Integrated Change Control provides status updates of change requests along with changes to the applicable elements of the Project Management Plan.

4.6 Close Project or Phase

This is the process of finishing all activities across the Project Management Process Groups to formally shutdown the project or phase.
The key question that must be answered is: has the project or phase delivered the requested results? Reviewing the Project Management Plan will indicate whether the current status of the project or phase deliverables justifies closure.
To be more precise, the project manager must ensure the following:

- Completion of all activities to meet the exit criteria for the phase or project;
- Completion of all activities to transfer the deliverables (product, service, result) to the next phase, or to the part of the requesting organization that will use, maintain and support those deliverables;
- Completion of all activities to capture project files and lessons learned for use by future projects.

Project files, lessons learned, historical information and templates are also known as Organizational Process Assets. These Organizational Process Assets are used by many processes in the knowledge areas.

Project closure needs to be done properly to prevent loose ends impacting the usage, maintenance or support of the project's result.

Chapter 5
Project Scope Management

The Project Scope is the answer to the 'what' question: what 'product' will the project deliver and what intermediate results needs to be produced to get the 'end product'.

Project Scope Management covers all processes in order to define and control the work that is needed and not needed to deliver the project result.

The Project Scope Management processes are:

1. Collect Requirements: defining and documenting stakeholders' needs to meet the project objectives;
2. Define Scope: creating a detailed description of the project and its product;
3. Create Work Breakdown Structure (WBS): breaking down project deliverables and project work into smaller, manageable components;
4. Verify Scope: getting the formal acceptance of the completed project deliverables;
5. Control Scope: monitoring the status of the project scope and controlling changes to the scope baseline.

The scope baseline consists of the project scope statement and the WBS. This scope baseline is then monitored, verified, and controlled throughout the lifecycle of the project (see figure 5.1).

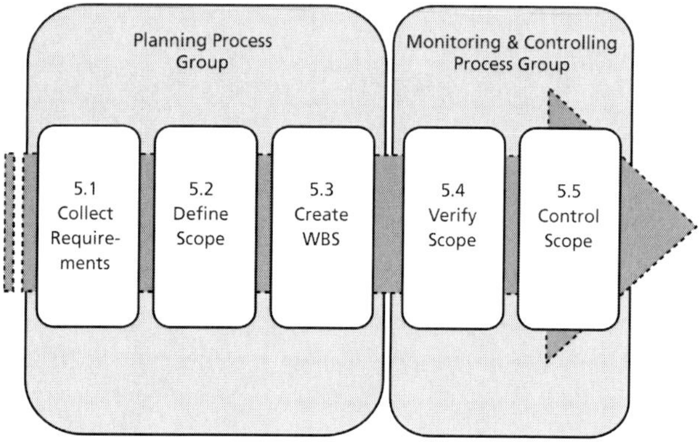

Figure 5.1 Overview of sections in Chapter 5 with Project Scope Management processes

5.1 Collect Requirements

Collecting requirements is all about defining and managing customer needs and expectations. Requirements are the foundation for the WBS. In addition the cost, schedule, and quality planning are all built upon these requirements. The development of requirements begins with an analysis of the information in the project charter and the stakeholder register.

The Project Charter contains the high-level project requirements that act as a foundation for the detailed product requirements. The Project Charter is described in Chapter 4.

The Stakeholder Register lists the stakeholders that can provide information on detailed project requirements. The Stakeholder Register is described in Chapter 10.

There are various techniques that can be used to collect the project requirements. Below you will find some examples.

Interviews

Interviewing project participants, stakeholders, and subject matter experts can provide valuable input for defining the features and functions of the project deliverables.

Facilitated workshops

Requirements workshops focus on stakeholders to help define project requirements. These facilitated sessions can improve relationships and trust among the participants which will contribute to increased stakeholder consensus.

Group creativity techniques

- Brainstorming: a technique used to generate and collect multiple ideas related to project and product requirements;
- Nominal group technique: this technique enhances brainstorming with a voting process used to rank the most useful ideas for further brainstorming or for prioritization.

Group decision making techniques

These techniques aim at reaching a group decision, for example:

- Unanimity: everyone agrees on a proposed way forward;
- Majority: proposal is supported by more than 50% of the members of the group;
- Plurality: the largest subset in a group decides even if a majority is not achieved.

Questionnaires and surveys

Techniques used to gather information, including statistics from a broad audience, with a relatively quick turnaround.

Observations

In cases where stakeholders have difficulty in articulating their requirements, observation practices such as 'job shadowing' (view how processes are being executed on-the-job) and participant observer ('perform the job yourself to experience the processes yourself') can help to establish the actual requirements.

Prototypes

The intention here is to implement a working model of the envisaged product or service to complete the requirements. Prototyping provides early feedback on requirements through the use of iterative cycles of creation, usage, feedback and prototype revision.

The products of the Collect Requirements process are the requirements documentation and the requirements management plan.

Requirements documentation contains individual requirements that are unambiguous (measurable and testable), traceable, complete, consistent, and acceptable to key stakeholders.

Examples of requirements documentation components are:

- Functional requirements, specifying business processes, information, and their interaction with each other;
- Non-functional requirements, such as service levels, performance, safety, security, compliance, supportability, etc.;
- Quality requirements;
- Acceptance criteria;
- Requirements assumptions and constraints.

The requirements management plan describes how requirements will be managed in terms of planning, tracking, reporting and prioritization.

5.2 Define Scope

Define Scope is the process of creating a detailed description of the project and product.

In order to define the scope the project manager will use the Project Charter and the requirements documentation. Both documents will provide the basic information to define the scope of the project.

Known techniques to support the creation of the project scope statement are the use of expert judgment and facilitated workshops.

The scope definition process will lead to the project scope statement.

The project scope statement documents the project's deliverables and the activities required to create those deliverables. It must also contain an explicit statement on all items that are excluded from scope in order to set the stakeholder expectations.

Based on the project scope statement the project team can undertake more detailed planning. In the case of requests for changes or additional work, the project scope statement will provide guidance to determine whether these requests are within or outside the project's boundaries.

The project scope statement includes:
- Product scope description: describes the product, service, or result to be delivered by its requirements;
- Product acceptance criteria;
- Project deliverables: deliverables include both the outputs related to the product or service of the project, as well as outputs such as project management reports and documentation;
- Project exclusions: deliverables being out-of-scope;

- Project constraints: describes all the project constraints that will limit the team's options, like, for example, a predefined budget or any imposed dates or schedule milestones that are issued by the customer or performing organization;
- Project assumptions.

5.3 Create Work Breakdown Structure (WBS)

Create WBS is the process of splitting project deliverables and their related project work into smaller, more manageable parts. PMI defines the work breakdown structure (WBS) as:

> A deliverable-oriented hierarchical decomposition of the word to be executed by the project team to accomplish the project objectives and create the required deliverables.

For specific information regarding work breakdown structures, we refer to the PMI's 'Practice Standard for Work Breakdown Structures – Second Edition'. This standard provides guidance for the generation, development, and application of work breakdown structures. It contains industry-specific examples of WBS templates that can be tailored to specific projects in a particular application area.

Both the project scope statement and the requirements documentation are the main inputs for creating the WBS, see figure 5.2.

The main technique for compiling a WBS is known as decomposition.

Decomposition is subdividing the deliverables into smaller, more manageable parts until the work and deliverables are defined to the work package level. This is the lowest level in the WBS. At this level the cost and activity durations for the work can be reliably estimated and managed.

WBS Example

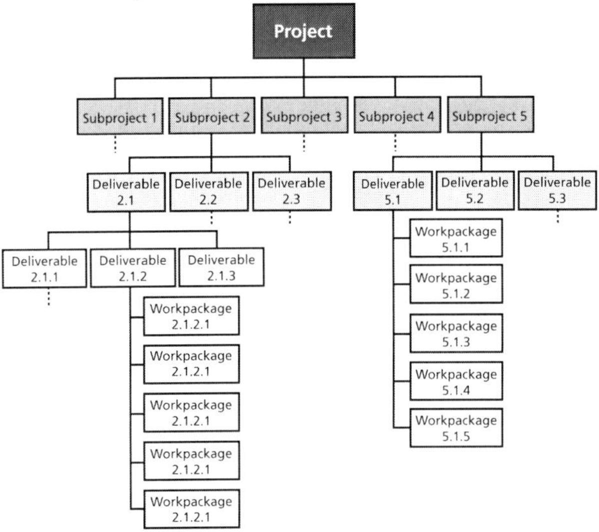

Figure 5.2 Example of WBS

Decomposing the work to greater levels of detail will enhance the ability to manage the work. However, excessive decomposition might lead to inefficiency in terms of managing, resourcing and performing the work.

The WBS is subject to what is sometimes called the 100% rule. The work packages at the lowest level must roll up to the higher levels covering all anticipated work in the project. The WBS must reflect all project work.

The WBS can be represented as an outline, an organizational chart, a fishbone diagram, or any other form of graphic.

Apart from the WBS itself, this process of creating the WBS will also result in the WBS dictionary and the scope baseline.

The WBS dictionary supports the WBS by providing detailed descriptions of the components in the WBS, including (amongst others):

- Description of work;
- Responsible organization;
- List of scheduled milestones;
- Resources required;
- Cost estimates;
- Quality requirements;
- Acceptance criteria.

The scope baseline consists of the following three components:

- Project scope statement;
- WBS;
- WBS dictionary.

5.4 Verify Scope

Verify Scope is the process to establish the formal acceptance of the completed project deliverable. It includes reviews of deliverables with the stakeholder to obtain their formal acceptance. The *PMBOK® Guide* makes a distinction between scope verification and quality control: '...scope verification is primarily concerned with acceptance of the deliverables, while quality control is primarily concerned with correctness of the deliverables and meeting the quality requirements specified for the deliverables.'

The project management plan, the requirements documentation and the validated deliverables will together enable the process of scope verification.

The project management plan, as described in Chapter 4, incorporates the scope baseline which consists of:

- Project scope statement;

- WBS;
- WBS Dictionary.

The validated deliverables are those deliverables that have been completed and checked for correctness by the Perform Quality Control process (see Chapter 8).

Scope verification will provide accepted deliverables and also change requests.

The accepted deliverables are the deliverables that are formally signed off and accepted by the applicable stakeholder. The formal stakeholder acceptance is forwarded to the Close Project or Phase process (4.6).

Those completed deliverables that have not been formally accepted usually need a change to elevate the deliverable to the required level for acceptance. The required change requests are handled through the Perform Integrated Change Control process (see Chapter 4).

5.5 Control Scope

Control Scope is the process of managing the project scope and the changes to the scope baseline. A fact of project life is that there will be changes to the scope. Since uncontrolled changes will lead to scope creep and introduce unacceptable risks, a strict change control process is required. Adhering to the Control Scope process will ensure that all scope changes are handled through the Perform Integrated Change Control process (see Chapter 4).

In order to control the scope, three products are needed: the project management plan, work performance information and the requirements documentation.

The project management plan contains the following components to control scope:

- Scope baseline;
- Scope management plan;
- Change management plan;
- Configuration management plan;
- Requirements management plan.

The work performance information provides data about project progress. It shows the status of each deliverable (started, in progress, completed, according to or not according to plan).

With all this information the project manager can check whether there is a difference between the work actually performed and scope baseline. In case of any differences, the project manager can propose corrective or preventive action if required by issuing change requests.

These change requests might lead to updates to the project management plan.

The project management plan updates are usually:

- Scope baseline updates;
- Other baseline updates: in case approved change requests have an effect on the project scope, then the corresponding cost baseline and schedule baselines might need revision to reflect the approved changes.

Chapter 6
Project Time Management

Time management is concerned with all the necessary steps to manage the timely completion of the project. Time management tries to determine feasible delivery dates, milestones or end dates, taking all known constraints into account. Time management is sometimes seen as the core discipline of project management and various popular software tools are available which mainly focus on the time management aspects. The printouts of these software packages are often called the 'project plan'. According to the Project Time Management knowledge area this is a 'project schedule' and not a project plan.

The 'Project Time Management' knowledge area covers six processes:

1. Define Activities;
2. Sequence Activities;
3. Estimate Activity Resources;
4. Estimate Activity Durations;
5. Develop Schedule;
6. Control Schedule.

If the project is of a smaller size, the different process steps can be executed in an integrated manner.

The way in which time management is executed in a defined project is outlined in the schedule management plan. This plan describes the approach taken on how the different time management techniques will be applied in the project, which software tool – if any – will be used, how effort and duration is calculated, what estimating techniques will be used and so on. The schedule management plan is part of the overall project management plan.

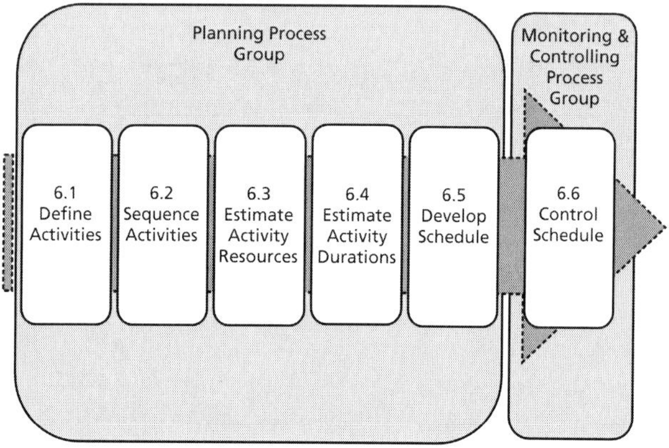

Figure 6.1 Overview of sections in Chapter 6 with the six Project Time Management processes

6.1 Define Activities

The first process defines the steps for creating the activity list from the work breakdown structure (WBS). All Project Time Management process steps are based on activities and not on WBS elements. A WBS (see Chapter 5.3) has decomposed the deliverables in the work packages. Activities, on the other hand, represent the work necessary to complete the work package. In smaller projects, however, there is not a clear distinction between activities and WBS elements.

The technique to define the necessary activities is called 'decomposition' and is completely identical to the technique described in Chapter 5.1.

Additionally, some activity attributes can be defined. Since time has passed since the development of the WBS, more details are known. Initial definitions of persons responsible, resource constraints, dependencies with other activities and first effort estimates can be documented.

6.2 Sequence Activities

After the activities have been identified in the previous process step, the project management team needs to come up with the correct order of execution, i.e. *which activity* has *what relationship* to other activities, which activity must come first, second, etc.

The result of this process step is a network diagram (see figure 6.2), showing the sequence of activities with mandatory (and preferred) relationships.

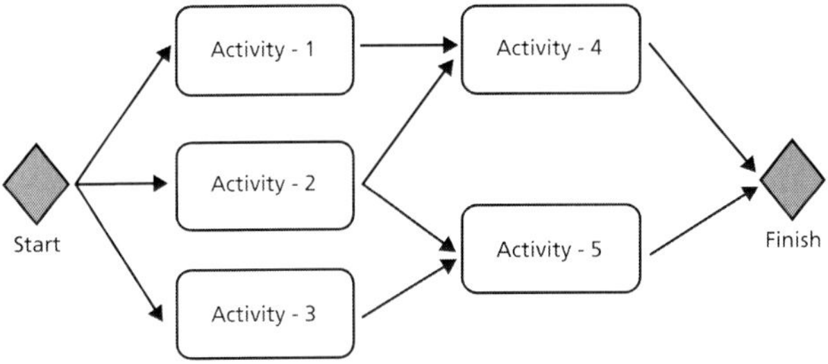

Figure 6.2 Network diagram

The first and most commonly used type of relationship is the Finish-to-Start dependency. Finish-to-Start means that the successor's start depends on the completion of the predecessor's activity.

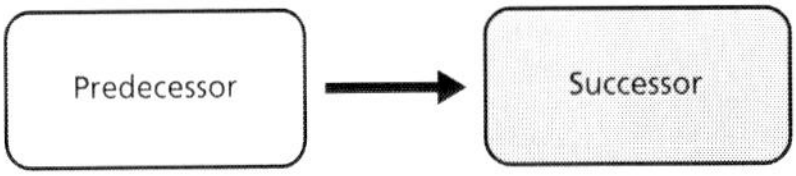

Figure 6.3 Finish-to-Start-relationship

There are more relationships between activities that can be defined:

- Finish-to-Finish: completion of the successor depends on the completion of the predecessor;
- Start-to-Start: start of the successor depends on the start of the predecessor;
- Start to Finish: completion of the successor depends on the start of the predecessor (this one is very tricky!).

It is very important to bear in mind the purpose of this process step Sequence Activities. It is to find and illustrate real dependencies. There are no resource constraints, and no effort estimates.

Example

If you go to a gas station, the 'Payment for the Gasoline' activity (PG) is a Finish-to Start relationship to the 'Fuel the Car' (FC) activity. The 'Check Tire Pressure' (CTP) activity is totally independent. Even if you are alone (i.e. the only available resource), the network diagram looks like the one in figure 6.4.

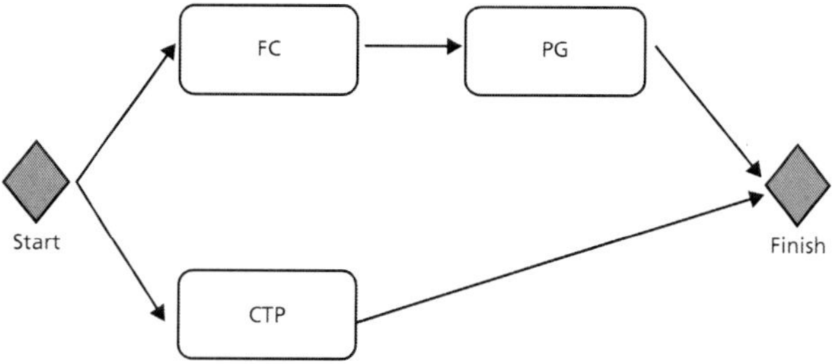

Figuur 6.4 Gas station network diagram

It is also important to note that each activity in a network diagram has an 'input arrow' and an 'output arrow'. The only two elements in a network diagram that have only one arrow are the Start Milestone (has only an output arrow) and the End Milestone (has only an input arrow). If an activity within a network diagram only has one arrow, it is an error and this activity is called a 'hanger'.

6.3 Estimate Activity Resources

The next step is to estimate the types and quantities of material, people, equipment or suppliers per activity. This is a tricky step, since the Estimate Activity Resource process will be a rough guess in the beginning and will be fine tuned during the Develop Schedule process.

The purpose is not only to come up with the estimated number of people but also to identify the right skills necessary (and other resources besides people) to do the job.

Example

A refurbishment project for a historical building may come up with a requirement to have specially trained painters available. In the first iteration of the process step we might identify the need for four of those painters in order to do the job. This is our first assumption, until the Develop Schedule process step shows that at least eight of them are needed to finish the project on time.

As a result, the activity resource requirements are identified and documented, a resource breakdown structure could be developed, and project documents, like the activity attributes, are updated.

6.4 Estimate Activity Durations

How long does an activity last? The answer to this question lies in the effort needed to fulfill the activity and the estimated available resources.

It is necessary to distinguish between effort and duration.
Effort is the work to be done. Duration is estimated work (effort) divided by estimated resources. Never confuse the two!

Example
The completion of 2,000 m^2 painted walls in a project is estimated to take 200 hours work for skilled painters; so this is the **effort** estimated for the job. The duration is dependent on the number of painters and their availability. With 10 painters – being the **estimated resources** - the **duration** is 20 working hours. When working 8 hours/day (= 8/24) the job could be finished in 2.5 working days.

In order to come up with an idea of the duration needed, the effort per activity needs to be determined. Activity effort estimation has been done either in the previous process step (Estimate Activity Resources) or in this process step. However, an estimation of duration without a proper determination of effort is impossible.

All estimates (effort or duration) have bigger variances (uncertainty) at the beginning of a project. Therefore, any estimates need to be progressively updated over the course of the project in order to decrease uncertainty and improve the project control.

There are several estimation techniques available. We will explain the most important three below.

Analogous estimating

This technique uses parameters like budget, size and complexity from previous projects. It is used when only a limited amount of information is available, typically in the early project phases. The danger of analogous estimating is in comparing two situations which actually shouldn't or might not be compared to each other. It is generally less costly but also less accurate.

Parametric estimating

It is similar to analogous estimating, but uses statistical relationships between historical (analogous) data and other estimating variables. A typical example of parametric duration estimating is the combination of time needed per square foot multiplied by total amount of square feet in a construction project. This technique can produce a higher level of accuracy based upon the sophistication and underlying data built into the model.

Three point estimate

This is considered to be one of the best methods for estimating. The three point estimate determines three values per activity:

- A most likely value (tm);
- An optimistic value (to);
- A pessimistic value (tp).

To determine the expected activity duration, the formula shown in figure 6.5 is used, weighting the most likely value by a factor of four.

$$\text{PERT} = \frac{\text{to} + (4*\text{tm}) + \text{tp}}{6}$$

Figure 6.5 Pert formula

This is proven to be one of the most efficient duration estimation techniques used in project management.

6.5 Develop Schedule

Now all the ingredients needed to develop the project schedule are ready to go. The activities are defined, the resources are estimated, the duration per activity is available and the logical relationships are defined in a network diagram. This development work is best done with a scheduling tool which will instantly produce a preliminary result based on the above developed inputs.

Developing a schedule is almost always an iterative process because first results seldom fit expected and agreed upon milestones or end dates.

The development of the schedule often requires review and revision of duration estimates and resource estimates.

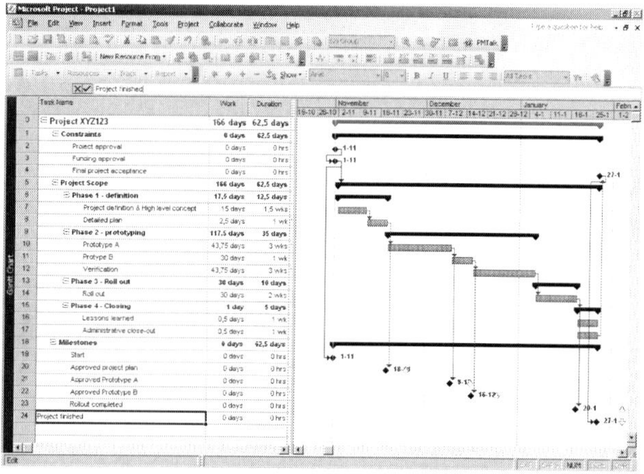

A developed schedule is subject to a schedule network analysis. This means that float and slack will be determined, the workload of the resources needs to be taken into account, what-if scenarios are executed, etc.

A well known method to analyze the schedule is called the **Critical Path Method** or **CPM**. Through using this method, the earliest possible end date is calculated by summing up the activity durations according to the network layout. CPM determines at least one path through the network diagram which will directly influence the end date. In other words, a delay on this route will most likely cause a delay of the next milestone. The CPM algorithm is the basis of most popular software packages and represents the standard in schedule development.

A relatively new technique is called **Critical Chain Method**. This method is based on CPM, but takes limited or very high specialized resources into account. After executing a normal CPM schedule, resource availability is entered and a resource-limited schedule result is determined. This resulting schedule often has a different critical path than the input schedule.

Resource leveling is a technique to deal with resources and to avoid an overload of work on a resource. Resource leveling is necessary when resources have been over-allocated or when a scarce resource is only available at certain times or in limited quantity.

Schedule compression using 'crashing' and 'fast tracking' is the next technique to deal with the project schedule. If the overall duration needs to be reduced, the project manager often uses one or both of these compression techniques. Crashing means that the duration of a single activity is shortened. How can this be accomplished? By adding resources or working overtime, for example. Fast tracking means that, for example, a successor activity in a finish-to-start relationship doesn't wait for the predecessor to finish but starts on its scheduled start date. Fast tracking increases the risk of rework, but is a commonly used technique to reduce project duration.

Typical results of the Develop Schedule process are project schedules as illustrated in figures 6.6, 6.7 and 6.8.

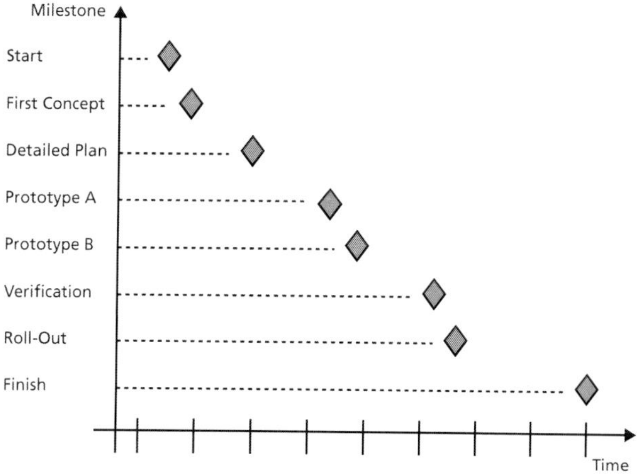

Figure 6.6 Milestone schedule

At the conclusion of Develop Schedule, the final result is the schedule baseline, which can be integrated in the overall project management plan.

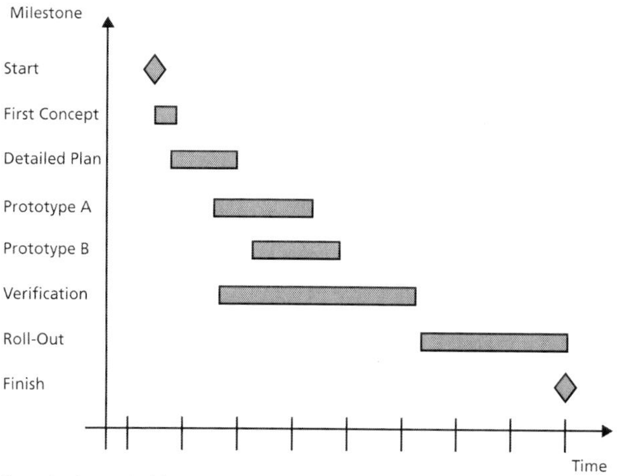

Figure 6.7 Gantt schedule

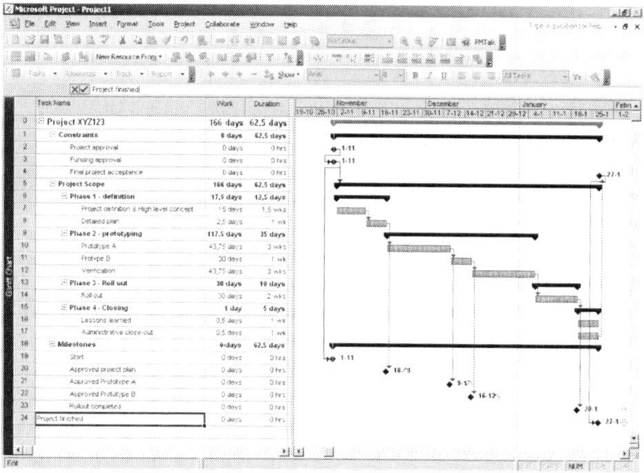

Figure 6.8 Project schedule: a detailed schedule with logical relationships

6.6 Control Schedule

One can easily imagine that without a schedule baseline it is impossible to control the schedule. But it is just as important to maintain this baseline in order to ensure that it continuously reflects the current situation. Therefore the process Control Schedule is used for monitoring the status and managing changes in the schedule baseline. It is concerned with:

- Determining the current status;
- Trying to influence factors which might cause schedule changes;
- Identifying if the schedule has changed for any reason;
- Managing the changes as they occur.

Ultimately this process results in both an updated project schedule and updated project records.

In conclusion, by systematically following these six logical project management processes for time management, the project manager, project management team, and senior management will be able to properly manage and communicate one of the most important project constraints: time!

This is the best way to proactively define and manage where on the timeline subsequent project deliveries could be achieved, thereby optimizing the duration aspect.

It is also invaluable in ensuring that activities are well planned and are right first time! This is of great value in maximizing the project outcome while minimizing the effort needed for that; thus optimizing the effort aspect.

As 'time is money', cost is mostly a consequence of how efficient we are able to manage time.

Chapter 7
Project Cost Management

Money is typically one of the key constraints of a project. Project Cost Management is therefore all about defining the budget and managing the actual project cost within the approved budget. But if the project's primary driver is financial, i.e. approved investment based on much higher expected savings after project delivery, it also about safeguarding and possibly improving the financial business case of the project.

In supplier-customer environments it is necessary to distinguish between the project budget and the potential price of a project (i.e. by selling the result of the project to the marketplace). Project management and especially Project Cost Management are only concerned with the budget – the price and the respective positive or negative margin is a management decision outside of the project. The elements of cost management are: defining the costs ('estimating'), building a baseline ('budgeting') and finally controlling the costs – mainly via an approach called Earned Value. This will be further explained in section 7.3.

The Project Cost Management knowledge area contains three processes:
1. Estimate Costs;
2. Determine Budget;
3. Control Costs.

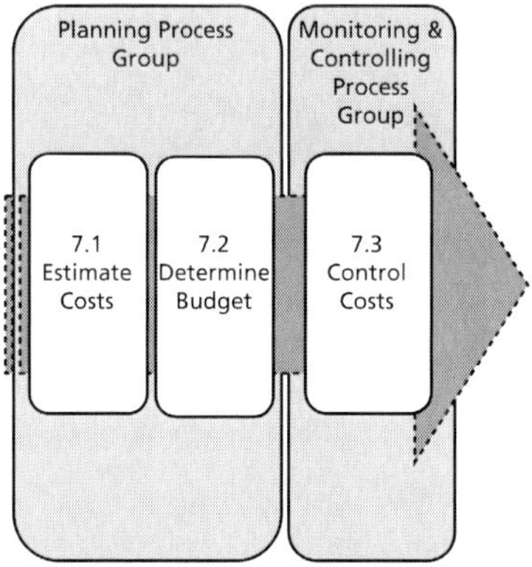

Figure 7.1 Overview of sections in Chapter 7 with the three Project Cost Management processes

A project manager needs to be aware of which costs are assigned to the project, how they are assigned and the concepts of controlling these costs. In the case where an IT project needs a dedicated test environment, it is crucial to have a clear view on the mechanics of how this test environment is budgeted. It is also very important to keep an eye on any stakeholder requirements for capturing costs. Different stakeholders may have different views and different requirements on how costs are assigned and reported.

Cost management is founded on early planning efforts, like scope definition and resource allocation. The approach on how costs will be managed in a given project is documented in a cost management plan. This plan, being part of the overall project management plan, describes all criteria necessary for planning, structuring, estimating, budgeting, and controlling project costs. A cost management plan should cover the following elements:

- 'Level of accuracy' – how precisely do we estimate and therefore control costs (rounding the data might be useful)?

- 'Units of measure' – what units do we use in our measurements (hours, weeks, days, months...)?
- 'Organizational procedure links' – how is the work in the WBS linked to the accounting system of the performing organization?
- 'Control thresholds' – which deviations from the baseline are considered to be normal and are allowed?
- 'Rules of performance measurements' – which rules do we apply in our project?
- 'Reporting formats' – what reporting format will our reports assume?
- 'Process description' – are there any additional process definitions to be accomplished?

Another aspect of project cost management covers the consequences of project decisions in respect to product maintenance or the cost of product support. Should we keep the project costs low in order to meet the budget, even if the result is increased maintenance costs?

7.1 Estimate Costs

Estimate Costs is not a one-time effort. In the early stages, or phases, of a project, the variances of estimates might be higher. The more information that is available, the better the estimates become. Therefore, cost estimates should be refined during the course of a project in order to narrow the range. The degree of uncertainty in the estimates depends on the product to be developed and might vary from industry to industry. Many organizations have guidelines in place as to what degree of accuracy is expected in which stage of the project.

Key message

When it comes to cost estimation, all resources that will be charged to the project will be part of that exercise: labor, materials, equipment, services, facilities and even inflation allowance or contingency costs.

At the end of this step all costs are estimated for all resources. It might be necessary to document the sources of the estimates as well, and to document the approach taken and the known constraints and assumptions which influenced the estimates.

Sources of input:

- The scope statement, WBS (including the WBS directory) and the list of activities - these are the most important elements in order to determine cost estimates;
- The project schedule - type and quantity of resources can be found here, as well as effort and duration estimates of the work to be done;
- Human resource plan - staffing attributes and personnel rates can be found here;
- Risk register - risk mitigation costs and potential (additional) costs in the event of risks occurring are documented here.

Taking the different inputs into account, the project team can make use of several tools and techniques to come to the best possible cost estimates in a given project phase. Some examples are given below.

First of all we have **expert judgment**. Guided by historical information from similar projects or work packages in the past, experts might have the best knowledge to combine methods of estimating and to reconcile differences between them.

Analogous estimating is similar to expert judgment. Information from other projects is used to determine the basis of the estimates for the current project.

Executive perspective

Analogous estimating is a gross value estimating approach, which is necessary and useful in early project phases, but could deliver surprising end results if not verified and subsequently replaced during the project by a more precise approach. Sufficient reserve should be accounted for when applying this technique.

Parametric estimating uses a mathematical model (like square feet in painting) to come up with a budget or duration, or even a price.

Project manager perspective
This approach needs a constant feedback loop from past experience to assure that the parametric model is valid and consistent. The project manager should never rely purely on computed figures, but should understand how this parameter is constructed, monitored and adjusted.

And finally there is **bottom-up estimating.** This is, in many cases, the most precise but also a very time consuming technique when it comes to cost estimating. This technique estimates the cost of each work package in a WBS element. Adding up the numbers of all work packages (lowest level) will result in an estimate of the overall project. This approach can even be more accurate by applying a '**three-point estimate**' technique. The three point estimate is discussed in section 6.4 and can also be applied to cost as well as to time.

7.2 Determine Budget

The project budget is derived from the aggregated cost estimates of the individual activities or work packages. The aggregated amount represents the budget of the project. However, any management reserves are not part of the project budget but remain under control of management.

By combining the estimates of the work packages or activities with the project schedule (i.e. the network diagram), a time-phased cost baseline will result. This baseline constitutes the funds authorized to execute the project and is a strong input to the next step 'Control Costs'.

Typically the baseline has the form of an S-curve, see figure 7.2. The cost baseline ('the S-curve') shows the amount of money to be spent over the course of the project. A second level of information pictured in this S-curve is the planned percentage of completion of the project's product. Thus, this S-curve is not only 'money spent' but also '(planned) work accomplished'.

Another result of the Determine Budget process is a project funding plan. If the project is funded with up-front customer payments, the baseline provides valuable input to any additional funding requirements or financial support of the performing organization.

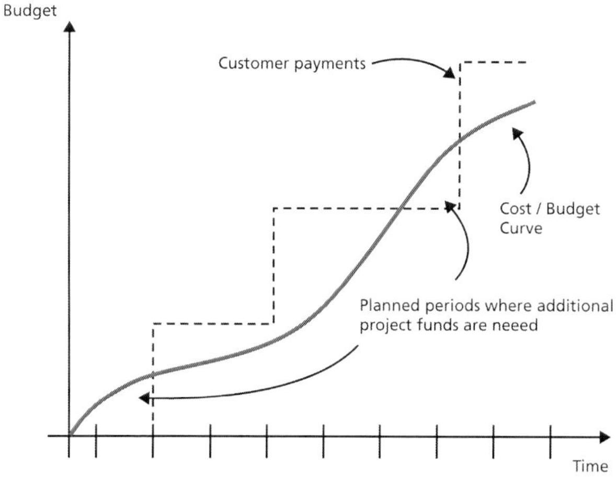

Figure 7.2 Example of an S-curve baseline

7.3 Control Costs

This process of the *PMBOK® Guide* contains one of the key project management controlling techniques used today. It is called Earned Value Management (EVM).

Control Costs is the process of monitoring the status of the project and is also used to manage changes to the cost baseline. Cost control includes influencing changes to the cost baseline, ensuring that all change requests are acted on in a timely manner, managing changes, and monitoring cost performance and work performance.

Two input elements are important to the Control Cost process. The first is the cost baseline, as discussed above (the S-Curve). The second is work performance information, i.e. the information about which work has been accomplished, which activities are completed and which activities or work

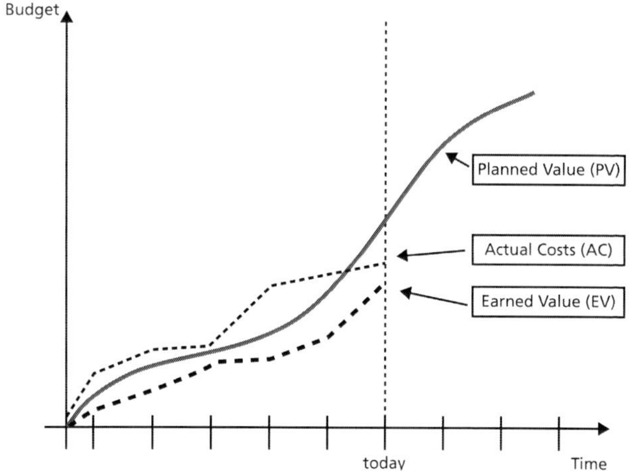

Figure 7.3 Earned Value

packages are currently in progress, and what amount of money or time has been spent.

A key element of cost and project control is the determination of the work accomplished. Different techniques and approaches are available to get the best possible view on the level of completion of the project. Key measurement words to watch for are called the 0/100 or 20/80 techniques.

Earned Value Management

As mentioned previously, Earned Value Management (EVM) is the key technique used to determine the current status of a project in terms of time and money. The rationale behind EVM is the comparison of the planned data ('the S-Curve') with the actual costs, and **independently** with the progress made by the team. The pure comparison between planned data and actual data might be totally misleading ("As of today we planned to spend $150k, and so far we have spent only $130k, we are $20k below our cost plan") because nothing is said on how the money was spent or whether the work completed is according to the plan. It is a pure assumption that the level of money spent is proportional to the work accomplished.

EVM introduces a third dimension by multiplying the budget with the percentage of the work accomplished. In the example above, let's assume the budget is $250k and the project manager reports a percentage completion of 40%. The virtual value of the project is $250k × 40% = $100k. The project has an 'Earned Value' of $100k. Of course, it is a fictional and virtual amount, since no-one will pay $100k for a half completed job. However, the Earned Value helps us determine our status in comparison to the money spent ($130k) and to the amount of money we should have spent as of today ($150k).

Given the numbers above, our project seems to be expensive. We have accomplished work to the value of $100k but have already spent $130k, so we are $30k over our planned cost.

And, given the numbers above, our project also seems to be late. We have completed work to the value of $100k but actually expected to have completed $150k's worth of work as of today. So we are $50k behind schedule. Yes, '$50k' behind schedule. This confuses almost every EV newbie: the time dimension is expressed in money units. But it makes the calculation simpler and everybody is aware of the fact: time is money...

Chapter 8
Project Quality Management

Project Quality Management supports the project in achieving its quality objectives.

The *PMBOK® Guide* recognizes the following three Project Quality Management processes:

1. Plan Quality: gathering all the quality requirements and describing how the project team will demonstrate its quality compliance.
2. Perform Quality Assurance: the process of auditing the application of the quality standards by reviewing the quality control measurements.
3. Perform Quality Control: executing the quality control activities to measure performance and recommend changes if needed.

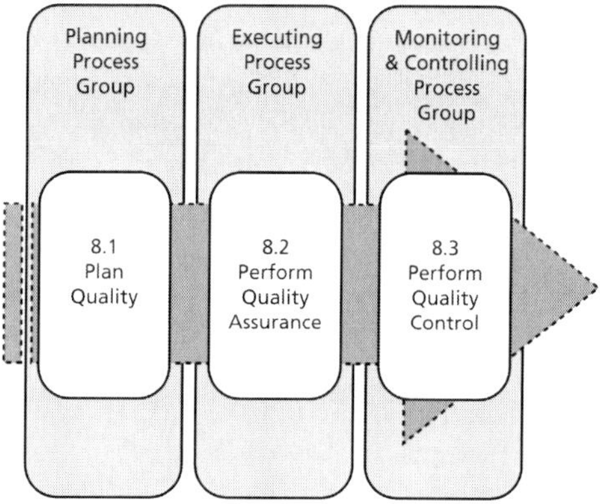

Figure 8.1 Overview of sections in Chapter 8 with the three Project Quality Management processes

Failure to meet the project's quality requirements will have a strong negative impact on project performance and the delivery of its expected result. This underlines the importance of quality management.

Quality can be defined as the level to which a product or service meets its specification or meets the expectations of its users. Quality is not synonymous to grade. Grade is an expression of a product's technical features. Two products or services can have the same functional use but can have a different number of features. Where low quality (many defects) is always a problem, low grade (limited number of features) may not be an issue.

Project management and quality management both acknowledge the importance of customer satisfaction, prevention over inspection, continuous improvement and management responsibility for quality.

The level of desired quality usually comes with a cost first, because of the effort needed to achieve it. This is a trade-off that project management and the sponsoring organization need to manage carefully because the cost of quality relates to the total product lifecycle and is not limited to the project lifecycle. Increasing quality as early as possible in the total lifecycle will lower the cost. Therefor we underline the statement: Quality is for free!

8.1 Plan Quality

The Plan Quality process aims to gather the project's quality requirements and to capture them in the quality management plan. The higher the quality requirements, the more time and money you may need to achieve the project result. Setting high quality standards may require a risk analysis on the impact to the project's plans. That is why Plan Quality is an integrated part of the project planning process.

Capturing the quality requirements starts with using the scope baseline to identify the quality requirements for the deliverables in scope. In case the organization uses its own quality policy, it is advisable to include this policy in the quality management plan.

The quality management plan should also identify the tools and techniques to be used for quality management. Examples of tools and techniques in this area are:

- Control charts: mainly used to determine the stability of process execution, using upper and lower specification limits to reflect maximum and minimum values allowed;
- Benchmarking: comparing results to those of similar comparable projects in order to set a basis for measurement;
- Design of experiments: defining the type and number of tests and their related costs;
- Statistical sampling;
- Other quality management methodologies like Six Sigma and Total Quality Management (TQM).

In summary: the quality management plan will describe how to assure and control quality.

On top of the quality management plan, you also need quality metrics for your quality control. A quality metric describes the test criteria for each deliverable.

8.2 Perform Quality Assurance

Quality assurance covers the audit process to ensure that the agreed quality standards and metrics are used by the quality control process. If gaps are found, the Perform Quality Assurance process will provide change requests for process improvement to increase the effectiveness and/or efficiency of the quality policies, processes and procedures. This might lead to updates, not only in the quality management plan, but also in the schedule and cost baseline due to the potential impact of process improvements to the project's cost and schedule.

8.3 Perform Quality Control

The *PMBOK® Guide* defines 'Perform Quality Control' as "…the process of monitoring and recording results of executing the quality activities to assess performance and recommend necessary changes."

Quality control reveals poor quality of project deliverables and the causes, and will make recommendations to improve quality whenever and wherever possible.

Executing the Perform Quality Control process is based upon the quality management plan and the quality metrics as described in section 8.1. Perform Quality Control exposes all project deliverables, to defined 'tests', the so-called 'quality control measurements'. The outcome of these measurements will either result in validated deliverables, rework, or in change requests. Once defects have been repaired by the project team, the related deliverables will be scrutinized again by the Perform Quality Control process. This cycle needs to be repeated until the deliverable has reached the status of 'validated deliverable' proving it has passed 'the test'.

Perform Quality Control will reveal defects (nobody is perfect!). Unless the time and money needed to repair those defects were covered by the initial cost and schedule baseline, these baselines will be subject to change.

The project management team should have working knowledge of at least the following basic tools of quality.

- Cause and effect diagram, also known as the Ishikawa diagram or fishbone diagram. This type of diagram is used to find the root cause of a problem by analyzing the underlying cause of each event that eventually will end up in 'the problem', See figure 8.2;

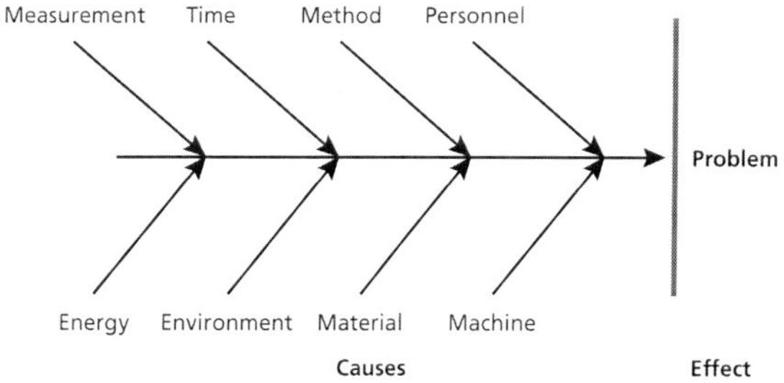

Figure 8.2 Cause and effect diagram

- Control charts: mainly used to determine the stability of process execution using upper and lower specification limits to reflect maximum and minimum values allowed;
- Pareto chart: this chart is a type of histogram that will show the frequency of various types of errors in order to focus the corrective action on the right type of error. This relates to Pareto's law also known as the 80/20 rule which basically translates to '80% of the total number of errors will be caused by 20% of the known causes.'

Other techniques used in quality control are:

- Statistical sampling (only testing a representative number of products);
- Inspection.

Chapter 9
Project Human Resource Management

Project Human Resource Management is about getting people on board the project and keeping, leading and managing them. These people are called 'project staff' or 'project team'. It is considered quite beneficial to have the project team assigned and available as early as possible – as their expertise will be used during the planning process and the commitment of the team towards the project will be strengthened.

The number of team members might change throughout the course of the project; it depends on the tasks and the work to be done. While the staff are needed for their particular project content-related expertise, the project manager's expertise is to orchestrate their roles and responsibilities, and to influence the project team in terms of communication, politics and organizational issues. In addition staff may be added to the team for specific project management support, like scheduling expertise, risk management expertise, or administrative support.

It is necessary to distinguish between the project team and the project management team. The latter is usually a subset of the project team, being concerned with typical project management activities. The project team is the sum of all people working for the project. There might be a programmer assigned 100% to a strategic IT project. If he or she is not involved in project management leadership activities, the programmer is not considered to be part of the project management team but rather of the project team.

The Project Human Resource Management knowledge area covers four processes:

- Develop Human Resource Plan;
- Acquire Project Team;
- Develop Project Team;
- Manage Project Team.

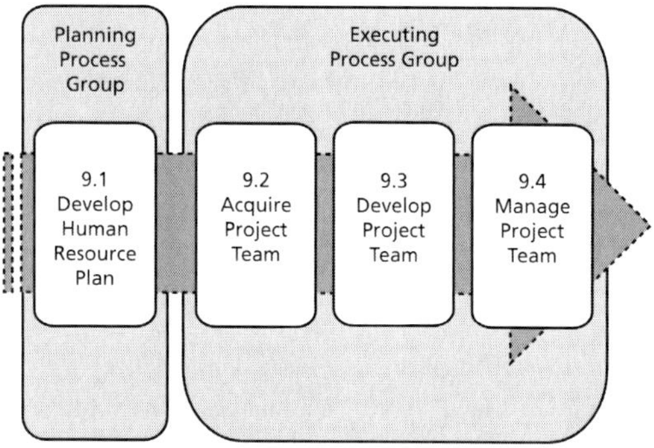

Figure 9.1 Overview of sections in Chapter 9 with the four Project Human Resource Management processes

9.1 Develop Human Resource Plan

The human resource plan is the documented approach on how, when and with whom the project needs to be staffed. A necessary prerequisite for developing this plan is a description of the required skills to fulfill the identified activities. Only if the activities are known and described, can a proper human resource plan can be set up.

The human resource plan defines the following elements, depending on the size of the project and the complexity of the product or the parties involved:

- Roles and responsibilities (always!);
- Required skills;
- Project organization chart;
- Timetable for staff acquisition and release;
- Training needs (if necessary) and team building strategies;
- ...and even more industry- specific elements like safety regulations or cultural issues.

A special focus should be on unique resources such as scarce technical experts or other limited human resources. It is not only necessary to describe the need to have Joe Bloggs, as he is the ultimate expert in a certain technology, available in June next year, but to also have covered the fact that Joe might not be around for several reasons. This might be an overlapping concern with risk management; however, the human resource plan should cover options to deal with this situation.

One of the classic tools to document roles and responsibilities is the RAM. RAM stands for 'responsibility assignment matrix' and is used to assign responsibilities to the project work. This can be done by a pure marker which indicates, who is responsible for what, or by using a role-based format like RACI. RACI are the first letters of: Responsible - doing the work; Accountable - end responsible; Consult - delivering input; and Inform - should be informed. These are used to indicate who in the team has which specific function on which activity, work package or deliverable.

Part of the human resource plan is finalizing the staffing management plan. Again, it depends on the project, its stakeholders and organizational environment how substantially this staffing management plan needs to be developed. However, especially in project situations which are decentralized, multi-cultural, matrixed or volatile in respect of expert availability, it might be a good idea to have a clear view on how to get the people in, how to deal with them and, importantly, how to release them at the end of the project.

	Peter	Paul	Mary	John
Activity 1	R	A	C	I
Activity 2			R	A
Activity 3	R	A		
Activity 4		A	R	I
Activity 5	R		C	A
Activity 6			R	A

Figure 9.2 Example of RACI scheme

9.2 Acquire Project Team

Acquire Project Team is the process of physically getting the project team members on board. It is not the planning process; it is the 'doing' or executing process of the human resource planning.

There are several techniques available to acquire the project team. They are either pre-assigned from an in-advance performed selection, or the project manager needs to negotiate for the resources with functional managers. Quite often the functional managers have previously promised delivery of resources to the project and only need to be reminded of their commitment. This is not the only area where project managers need to prove that they have strong negotiation and communication skills. Even if the delivery is documented and confirmed in a human resource plan or in the staffing management plan, the world has usually done some turns and the situation for the stakeholders might have changed. Insisting on the execution of a previously signed document does little to help either party.

If no internal staff are available for the required skill-set, project team members need to be acquired via an outside source. Whether or not the project manager is authorized to conduct procurement processes should have been defined in the human resource plan.

Virtual teams are a relatively new approach to forming project teams. Due to new opportunities offered by remote communication, a project team can be comprised of a group of people, who seldom or never meet face-to-face. However, special attention must be given to effective communication and to ensure team members remain on the same wavelength.

9.3 Develop Project Team

This process is about improving competencies, team interaction and the overall team environment. It is the process of transforming a group of people into a team, since (real) teamwork is a critical factor for project success. The necessity to develop an effective project team is a key responsibility of the project manager. Successful team performance is achieved by:

- Using open and effective communication;
- Developing trust among team members;
- Managing conflicts in a constructive manner;
- Encouraging collaborative problem solving and decision making.

Team performance can be measured by using team performance assessments. These assessments can reveal interesting correlations between achieving the project results on the one hand and the team performance in terms of conflicts, leadership, openness, trust, etc. on the other.

A project manager should not be afraid to continuously conducting a team performance assessment throughout the project lifecycle.

A highly performing team is characterized by results-oriented outcomes. To improve their performance, specific training, coaching, and mentoring needs might be identified.

As a result, not only project results are more likely to be achieved, but also positive side effects are attained. These side effects could be:

- Skill improvement leads to higher effectiveness;
- Improvement in competencies help the team perform better;
- Lower staff turnover rate;
- Better team cohesiveness.

A key technique for better team performance is the understanding of team development phases, a classic approach described by Tuckman. Each team goes through a number of stages and each stage is linked to better or worse team performance. The path through those stages is not a one-way street, a team can get caught in one stage or can slip backwards into an earlier stage. However, well-oiled teams tend to skip one stage (or at least overcome the drawbacks of some stages faster).

The *PMBOK® Guide* defines five stages.

1. Forming – the team meets and learns about its roles and responsibilities. There is usually high respect towards the group, a big safety clearance, but the team is not yet high performing.
2. Storming – the safety clearance tends be reduced by the initial team members. Reasons for that are multifaceted, usually due to different personalities, different skills and different experience. As a result, performance goes down and conflicts arise.
3. Norming – personalities and work habits get adjusted. Ground rules are established or fine tuned. The team begins to trust each other. If

'Norming' is not executed properly, the 'Storming' phase can smolder and poison the whole team.

4. Performing – the work is done smoothly and effectively. The team performance is at an optimum level. Every team would like to be in this phase; however, there is no direct access by jumping over the preceding phases.
5. Adjourning – work is completed and the team moves on.

Special attention must be given to the 'Storming – Norming' curve. There are a number of experiments documented which show that a direct move towards 'Performing' is almost impossible. Effective teams also go through 'Storming – Norming', but much faster. So the question is not 'How to avoid Storming?' but rather 'How fast can we start Norming?'

9.4 Manage Project Team

Now, after the team members had been acquired and developed, the project team needs to be managed in terms of performance and issue resolution. This process requires a variety of general management skills. Special emphasis is required on communication, conflict management, negotiation, and leadership, as well as on setting challenging assignments for the project staff and on providing recognition when achieving the desired results.

The outcome of this process is a well managed project team led through the ups and downs of the project.

Typical techniques to manage project teams are outlined below.

- Observation and conversation – nobody can manage a team without working closely with the people. This does not necessarily mean physically close. Remote team members can also be closely linked to the project work;

- Performance appraisals – helps to identify unknown or unresolved issues;
- Conflict management – conflict is inevitable in a project environment. The question is not 'How to avoid conflicts' but rather 'How to deal with conflicts correctly'. The better the conflict resolution technique is, the better the expected project results. Conflicts need to be addressed with different conflict resolution techniques, where each technique has its own place and use, depending on the situation, culture, circumstances and objectives. Commonly used techniques include: Withdrawing and/or Avoiding, Smoothing, Compromising, Forcing, Collaborating, Confronting and Problem Solving;
- Interpersonal skills – are needed to analyze situations and interact appropriately. There is a wide range of interpersonal skills necessary to manage the project team. An appropriate use of these skills helps the project manager to achieve project goals and objectives:
  - Leadership;
  - Team building;
  - Motivation;
  - Communication;
  - Influencing;
  - Decision making;
  - Political and cultural awareness;
  - Negotiation.

In conclusion, the well structured application of human resource management processes results in the project manager being more likely to ensure that the right people are on board. The next step is leading this team successfully to the level where the project manager can allow a more facilitating style as people are working together in the right spirit and demonstrating excellent team performance. One should never forget: project work is no routine job - it demands the commitment and drive of the people working at it!

Executive perspective

Executive and line management play an important role here in continuously balancing the project resource needs with the needs of the line organization and clearly setting the priorities. A culture where project work is viewed as 'next to my real job' and done 'when we have time left' quickly diminishes project team member commitment as well as resulting in unpredictable resource availability.

Project manager perspective

Project managers, together with project team members, should reinforce the proactive communication about commitments made and the outcomes delivered accordingly. Challenges will be there, more than in a line organization, as projects have much more uncertainty. Finger pointing will never solve problems. Cooperation and a focus on creating solutions together is an essential attitude for teams that strive to consistently demonstrate top performances.

Chapter 10
Project Communications Management

Effective communication enhances the project's chance of success by building stakeholder relationships that can be leveraged to create coalitions and partnerships. It creates bridges between diverse stakeholders involved in a project, and connects various cultural and organizational backgrounds, different levels of expertise, and various perspectives and interests in the project execution or outcome. Project managers spend most of their time communicating or facilitating, and ensuring communication between stakeholders. This starts from day one of the project!

Project Communications Management defines the key processes required to ensure timely and appropriate exchange of project information. The related processes should be periodically reviewed during the project lifecycle and adjusted in the light of any changes that have occurred.

The Project Communications Management knowledge area has five processes:

1. Identify Stakeholders.
2. Plan Communications.
3. Distribute Information.
4. Manage Stakeholder Expectations.
5. Report Performance.

A basic principle of communication is the so called 'sender-receiver' model. Information is sent and received between two parties, one of them being the sender and the other the receiver. Information from the sender towards the receiver needs to be encoded (thoughts and/or ideas are translated in a language), resulting in a message. The message is the output of encoding

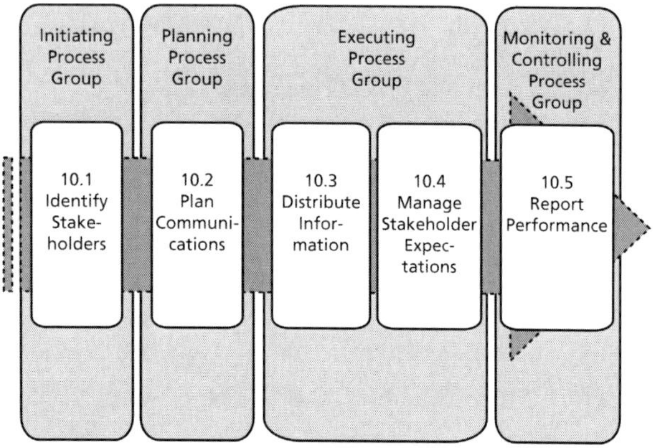

Figure 10.1 Overview of sections in Chapter 10 with the five Project Communications Management processes

and is sent to the other party via a medium (the method used to convey the message). The receiver decodes the message by translating it into meaningful thoughts, see figure 10.2.

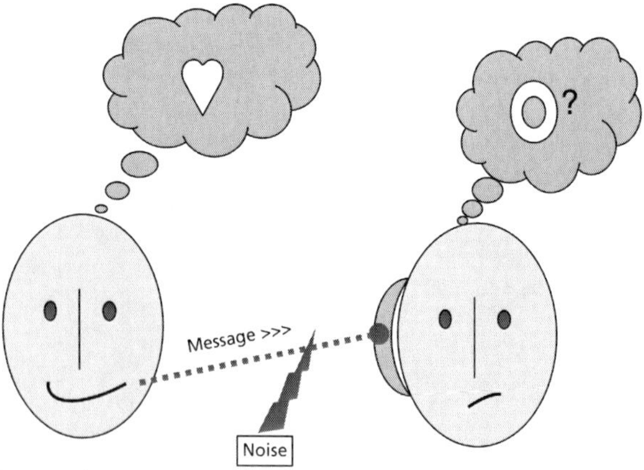

Fig 10.2 Sender-receiver communication model

During the path from encoding, message delivery and decoding, a disturbance or a noise can occur. This noise is not only limited to the physical message delivery but also to encoding or decoding due to different encoding/decoding algorithms. Encoding and decoding can be influenced by culture, education, language, and social background.

As part of the communication process, the sender is responsible for sending the message clearly and completely, and for confirming that it is properly understood (feedback). The receiver is responsible for making sure that the information is received completely, understood correctly and acknowledged (also feedback).

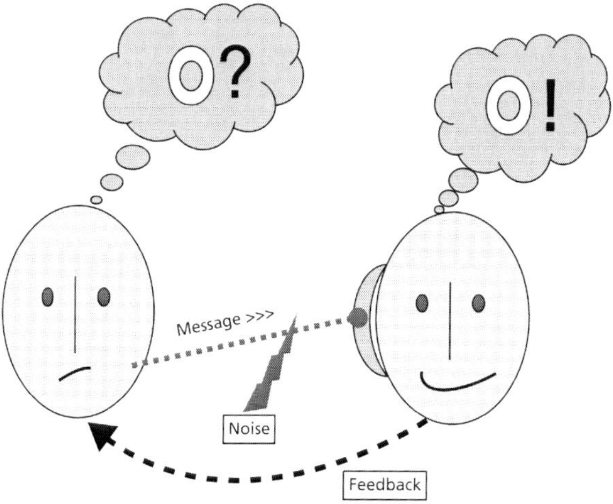

Figure 10.3 Feedback as part of the communication process

10.1 Identify Stakeholders

Project stakeholders are persons and organizations that are actively involved in the project, or whose interests may be positively or negatively affected by the execution of the project and/or the implementation of the project result. Because they may exert influence over the project and its deliverables, it is essential to identify them in order to be able to deal with them in a proactive manner.

Failing to identify key stakeholders and their requirements will increase timelines and cost, lower the quality of the end result, affect acceptance levels and therefore project success. By not identifying a stakeholder you 'only' miss out 100% of their requirements in this phase. Also when a stakeholder is identified much later in the project lifecycle – e.g. during implementation and transition – it will in most cases cause them to have negative interests and expectations towards the project, as well as being reluctant to perform any project-related work.

As project management is all about communications, it is critical for project success that the stakeholders are identified as early as possible in the project in order to plan appropriate communications relating to their potential interest in the project.

The key technique in this process is called the 'stakeholder analysis'. After performing a stakeholder analysis, a set of stakeholders are identified and captured in a stakeholder register. Depending on criticality, influence and impact, stakeholder management strategies need to be developed in order to increase support and decrease any negative impact.

Stakeholder analysis

As most projects will have a large number of stakeholders and time is limited, stakeholders need to be classified to ensure a structured focus on the most important relationships that will help to ensure a successful delivery of the project's product, as well as its smooth transition into operations. A stakeholder analysis supports the project management team in quickly creating a better understanding. This assessment should be periodically reviewed to adjust for potential changes. Stakeholder analysis generally follows three steps.

Stakeholder Register for Charlie's 17th Birthday				
Stakeholder	**Examples**	**Expectation**	**Power (Scale 1 – 3)**	**Interest (Scale 1 – 3)**
The Birthday Kid	Charly	Good party, cool games	3	3
Neighbors, not invited	Mr. Jones	House access still possible, end @ 10:pm	2	1
Musicians	The Moodys	New customers	1	2
Guests with Kids	Ann and Mike	Alternative offerings	2	3
Guests Core Team	Paul, Thomas, Anton and Bart	Early information, appreciated contribution	3	3

Figure 10.4 Example of a stakeholder register

- Step 1: Identify all potential project stakeholders and relevant information, such as their roles, departments, interests, knowledge levels, expectations, and influence levels.
- Step 2: Identify the potential impact or support each stakeholder could generate, and classify them so as to define an approach strategy. In large stakeholder communities it is important to prioritize the key

stakeholders to ensure the efficient use of effort to communicate and manage their expectations. Helpful classification models are:

- power/interest grid, grouping the stakeholders based on their level of authority ('power') and their level or concern ('interest') regarding the project's outcomes;
- power/influence grid, grouping the stakeholders based on their level of authority ('power') and their active involvement ('influence') in the project;
- influence/impact grid, grouping the stakeholders based on their active involvement ('influence') in the project and their ability to effect changes to the project's planning or execution ('impact');
- salience model, describing classes of stakeholders based on their power (ability to impose their will), urgency (need for immediate attention), and legitimacy (their involvement is appropriate).

- Step 3: Assess how key stakeholders are likely to react or respond in various situations, in order to plan how to influence them to enhance their support and mitigate potential negative impacts.

The Executive perspective

Project Communications Management is one of the areas where executives play an important role. Active involvement by senior management in continuous communication on the project's business case (it's the sponsor's business case!), as well as close communication with the project manager is key. It takes two to tango.

Be aware of the right 'power balance'. Too detailed involvement increases the risk of 'taking over' (micro management) the project manager's role, or even a team member's role, as no one dares to challenge senior management out of respect for their hierarchical position.

10.2 Plan Communications

Who needs what kind of information, when will they need it, how will it be given to them, and by whom? The answers to all these questions can be found in a communication management plan, which is the result of this process step.

It is not sufficient to send out a monthly report in the standard format. Depending on the communication needs of the various stakeholders, communication needs to be planned and agreed. In a case where the CFO of a company is one of the core stakeholders of the project, perhaps due to challenging project funding, he or she will appreciate precise and concise financial information. This report might be totally different from the report to the engineering department. They are less interested in financial figures but more so in changes of the product's blueprint.

A communication management plan defines:

- Communication requirements of the various stakeholders;
- Information to be distributed, including language, format, content and level of detail;
- Time frame and frequency;
- Person responsible;
- Methods used to convey the information: memo, e-mail or press release;
- Self organizational process definition, for items such as an escalation process, method for updating, flow chart of information flow, guidelines and templates for status meetings, etc.

A nuclear plant refurbishment project will obviously have different stakeholders and different communication needs than a software release update project. But the communication plan is the essential tool to provide a clear strategy for communication on every project. Factors that can affect the project's communication include:

- Urgency of the need of communication;
- Availability of technology;
- Project staff knowledge on communication tools;
- Duration of the project;
- Environmental factors such as virtual teams.

10.3 Distribute Information

As communication has been planned in the previous step, this process is about distributing the appropriate information to the various stakeholders. It is not only the implementation of the communication plan and the communication needs described in the stakeholder analysis, it is also about responding to unexpected requests for information.

There is a variety of tools available to distribute information, such as electronic communication (e-mail, fax, voice mail, phone, video, web conferencing) followed by hard copy document distribution (press releases) and finally specialist solutions and tools for project management (web interfaces for project management software, virtual office support software, portals and collaborative work management tools).

Information distribution is not only limited to sending out information. Information can also be distributed via a presentation, and presentation techniques should be considered as a valuable technique for information distribution. The same goes for a professional writing style, meeting management techniques and the choice of media.

Finally, the distributed information can be classified into roughly six types:

- Stakeholder notifications with resolved issues, approved changes and general project status;
- Project reports, both formal or informal;

- Project presentations to different groups of stakeholders, that can be of varying length and complexity;
- Project records, ranging from memos, correspondence and meeting minutes to (also legally) documenting project progress and recording the foundation for decisions;
- Feedback from stakeholders to improve performance;
- Lessons learned documentation that will become part of the historical database and help to improve future performance.

10.4 Manage Stakeholder Expectations

This process is about influencing expectations of the stakeholders, addressing concerns and resolving issues.

It is not enough to analyze the expectations and needs of the stakeholders, those expectations need to be actively managed in order to meet the needs of the stakeholders and to address issues as and when they occur.

There are no special tools and techniques that assist in managing the expectations of the stakeholders other than general management skills and general interpersonal skills.

It is less a matter of tools but more a matter of constantly being aware of the stakeholders, their expectations in terms of communication and results, their concerns and their attitude towards the project.

As a result of this activity, change requests could be created and should be handled through the standard change request process. Updates are also expected on the stakeholder register itself, the issue log and, potentially, the documented stakeholder management strategy.

10.5 Report Performance

The last process in the communication knowledge area is Report Performance. Some project management specialists consider this process as a part of the Distribute Information process, but it stands as a discrete process in the *PMBOK® Guide*. Without question, performance reporting is a crucial element and should follow the overall communication management plan.

The typical performance report is a simple status report using traffic light indicators to show potential divergences. More elaborate reports may include:

- Status dashboards for each area;
- One page scorecard systems;
- Analysis of past performance;
- Current status of risks and issues;
- Work completed and percentage completed;
- Change situation and statistics;
- Any other relevant information which should be reported.

A complete status report covers the past ('How did we do'), the present ('What is our current status') and the future ('This is our forecast for the objectives'). Special attention is necessary to take the stakeholder preferences into account and decide which of the three elements is the most important one.

Sponsors and steering boards are usually more interested in the future ('forecasting methods') and/or in a profound analysis, such as why the project deviated from the plan ('variance analysis').

Variance analysis

Variance analysis is an after-the-fact look at what caused a difference between the baseline and the actual performance. When comparing the project baseline data with the actual information of a project, both differences (favorable and unfavorable) need to be noted. A really useful technique for quantifying cost and schedule variances is the Earned Value Method (EVM).

The impact of the differences needs to be determined and shown.

Forecasting methods

Using forecasting methods is an attempt to predict future project performance based on the actual performance to date.

Four categories of forecasting methods are available.

- Time series methods – historical data is used to predict future outcomes. Earned Value Estimate At Completion and Estimate To Complete are an example of that, also moving average, extrapolation and trend analysis;
- Causal/econometric methods – these forecasts use a correlation between two factors such as umbrella sales and weather conditions. If the causes are understood, projections of the influencing variables can be made;
- Judgmental methods – intuitive judgments, opinions and probability estimates are used;
- Others like simulation, probabilistic forecasting and ensemble forecasting.

Chapter 11
Project Risk Management

Projects are by definition a 'risky' endeavor. It means dealing with unknown situations. In order to prevent each project becoming a 'game of chance', Project Risk Management can support us in controlling the project risks. Project risks are future uncertainties that may affect project results – in both directions, i.e. for the better or worse. Project risks are not business risks, or risks that are related to the performing organization. A project might create such risks, but they are handled from a different perspective.

Risks are uncertainties that matter. It is the job of the project management team to take care of those uncertainties, to identify them, to analyze their impact, to develop responses, if applicable, and to monitor and control their effect.

If the project management team neglects risk management, it will be constantly faced with problems on the one hand and missed opportunities on the other. Risk management is about trying to minimize the impact of potential threats on project results, which is usually everything that could cause a project to be delayed, be more expensive, or be delivered with less quality. Risk management on the other hand is also about trying to maximize the impact of potential opportunities; factors which help to achieve the project results faster, cheaper and with better quality. These need to be actively promoted and supported.

The "Project Risk Management" knowledge area has six processes:
1. Plan Risk Management.
2. Identify Risks.
3. Perform Qualitative Risk Analysis.

4. Perform Quantitative Risk Analysis.
5. Plan Risk Responses.
6. Monitor and Control Risks.

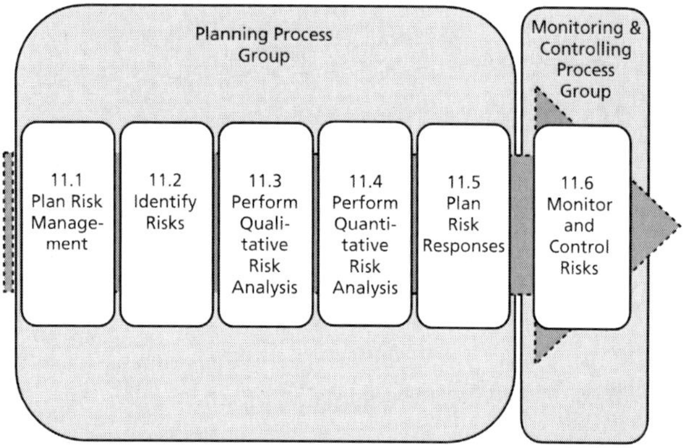

Figure 11.1 Overview of sections in Chapter 11 with the six Project Risk Management processes

Risk management processes are worthless if they are performed only once, say at the beginning of the project. Constant evaluation is necessary to really harvest the full benefits of risk management.

11.1 Plan Risk Management

This process creates a risk management plan. You will not find a single risk in the management plan. It is the management plan on how the project team will perform risk management for the given project. It is a clear and unambiguous plan defining all risk-related details, tools, techniques, stakeholder preferences etc. in this particular project setting. If a detailed risk methodology is in place, the risk management plan may be very small in size – only defining the particularities of the project ('We meet every Wednesday in room 345, 3rd floor'). If the risk methodology in the performing organization is less mature and developed, the risk management plan tends to become correspondingly larger in size and volume.

The following elements need to be defined.

- Methodology – which approach, tools and data will be adopted to perform risk management?
- Roles and responsibilities – who will be doing what in risk management? These are important definitions which need to be defined upfront. When handling emergency risk situations, the roles and responsibilities need to be crystal clear;
- Budgeting – how are risks budgeted throughout the project? Is a different budgeting approach in place for quantified risks, qualified risks and unknown risks? What is the budgetary implication of contingency reserves?
- Timing – how often will the risk process cycle be performed during the project and how are the risk management activities incorporated into the overall project schedule?
- Risk categories – do we have predefined risk categories, i.e. sources of risk which can be linked to identified risks or even help to identify risks? An important tool to help define risk categories is a risk breakdown structure (RBS). However, a risk breakdown structure is a structure of potential risk sources. The risks to the project are not embedded in the RBS;
- Definitions of risk probability and impact – this part of the risk management plan is to ensure that all project stakeholders have a common understanding of what is meant by a specific risk description. For example, if a risk is termed 'medium', then without any prior definition there might well be ten different meanings for ten team members;

- Probability and impact matrix – how do we illustrate the risk exposure of the project and which format will be used?
- Revised stakeholder tolerances – if there is a need to revise stakeholder tolerance then this is the right place to document it;
- Reporting formats – how do we report the risk situation and what format will be used?
- Tracking – documents how risk activities will be recorded for the benefit of the current project.

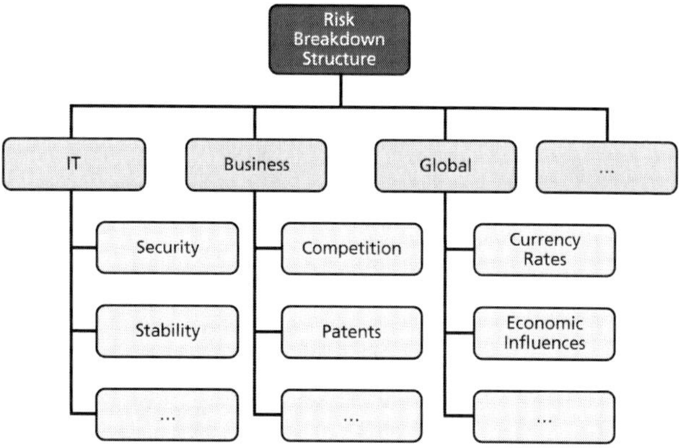

Figure 11.2 Example of a risk breakdown structure (RBS)

11.2 Identify Risks

This is the process used to determine which risks may influence the objectives of the project. The step is purely about risk identification, i.e. to find the risk, to document the risk and to describe the impact of the risk should it occur. The results are captured in a list called the 'risk register'.

At the end of the process, a new or updated risk register is available. However, the project team should focus on describing the risk in a correct manner, using correct syntax. It makes absolutely no sense to respond to risks which are not described correctly.

Remember: risks are uncertainties, which relate to project results. If there are no effects on objectives – then there are no risks!

Example

How about this register entry 'The traffic is a risk'? This is wrong in that the traffic is not a risk in itself. However, it might become a source of some type of risk. Correct syntax could be something like:

'Because of heavy traffic in the morning hours (fact), it is likely I will get stuck in a traffic jam and miss the airplane, the result being I will have no chance to demonstrate the new XYZ model to the customer (uncertainty) with the effect that I won't be able to meet my sales targets (impact on objectives)'.If the risks are correctly described, we start getting a chance to manage them.

Identifying risks is based on project documents, past experience and technology used. It is critical to not only concentrate on technical (product) risks, but also on process (project) risks.

The identification itself can be done through different techniques:

- Brainstorming – the most common approach when it comes to collecting risks;
- Delphi technique – unlike brainstorming, experts are independently and anonymously interviewed in various iterations. The Delphi technique is used to avoid personal influences;
- Interviewing (ask the experts!);
- Root cause analysis – a technique used to develop preventive action to a known problem.

The most common tool to build a risk register is spreadsheet software like Microsoft Excel or something similar. An advantage of this solution is that all subsequent activities can be stored in the same spreadsheet.

11.3 Perform Qualitative Risk Analysis

A qualitative analysis is an assessment of the identified risks for further analysis and quick prioritization. A qualitative analysis can be done rather quickly and allows a good overview of the risk portfolio and exposure. Combining probability of occurrence and impact on objectives creates a matrix which is known as the 'probability and impact matrix'.

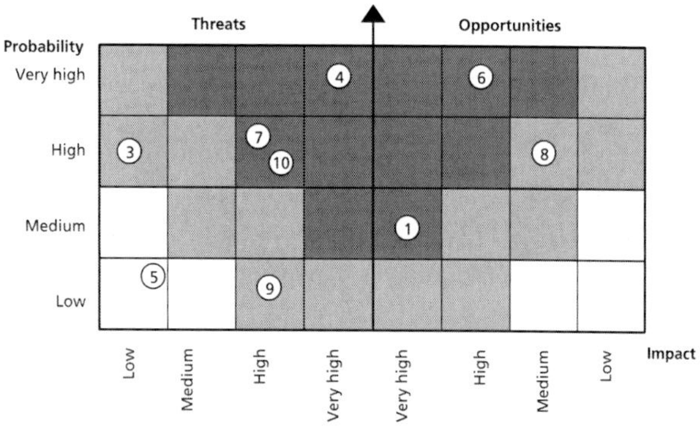

Fig 11.3 Probability and impact matrix

Figure 11.3 shows two matrices. The left hand side is for threats (negative risks) and the right hand side is for opportunities (positive risks).

The big advantage of this process step is that it can be executed quite quickly. The drawback, however, is that nobody knows how big 'small' is, or what the real impact is of something called 'high'.

Don't confuse 'qualitative risk analysis' with risks on quality. These are two separate things, independent from each other.

11.4 Perform Quantitative Risk Analysis

With this step some risks (usually the 'biggest', either positive or negative) will be numerically analyzed. For example, instead of probability being 'small' and impact 'high', this process tries to come up with concrete values such as probability is 5% and impact is \$34.000. Determining or trying to determine the exact numbers is much more precise but involves a lot of effort. Availability of time and budget, together with the need for quantitative figures, will determine to what extent a quantitative analysis is executed.

Techniques to carry out the quantitative risk analysis are:

- Interviewing and brainstorming - still the biggest source of quantitative data by just using paper and pencil, historical information and the past experience of subject matter experts;
- Probability distributions – continuous probability distributions, used extensively in modeling and simulation represent the uncertainty in values such as durations of schedule activities and costs of project components;
- Sensitivity analysis – tries to determine the influence of one variable in a multi-variable environment;
- Expected monetary value analysis – a technique to combine different values and different probabilities in one expected monetary value. If you buy a lottery ticket for \$10 and the chance of wining the main price of \$1.000 is 5%, the expected monetary value is 5% * \$1.000 = \$50

minus the investment of $10 = $40. The expected monetary value is artificial, since you win either $1.000 or nothing. But it is very helpful to determine a value based on probability;

- Monte Carlo Simulation – the best way to determine schedule uncertainties and influence of probability distributions to a project schedule.

11.5 Plan Risk Responses

After the risks are identified and analyzed, it is time to determine a strategy on how to deal with the risks captured in the risk register. Risk responses are actions which will be taken in advance in order to deal with the risk accordingly.

There are four possible responses for either threats or opportunities. Let's start with the threats:

- Avoid - means to set probability or impact on zero. If the probability is set to zero the risk will never occur, whilst if the impact is zero the risk might occur but does not impact objectives. Often used when probability and impact is high;
- Mitigate – probability or impact is lowered, but not set to zero. Please note that the chance of the risk might be lower, but it still exists;
- Transfer – the risk is transferred to a third party;
- Accept – the risk is identified, analyzed and accepted, i.e. nothing will be done to lower probability or impact.

Strategies for opportunities are:

- Exploit – if the organization wants the opportunity to occur;
- Share – as with 'transfer', the ownership of the risk is given to a third party which is best able to capture the opportunity or the benefit;
- Enhance – probability or impact will be increased;
- Accept – the opportunity is identified, analyzed and accepted, i.e. nothing will be done to increase probability or impact.

11.6 Monitor and Control Risks

The final process step in this chain is actually 'risk management'. All planning steps prior to Monitor and Control Risks are necessary to really start working with risk management.

Risk response plans are implemented, identified risks will be tracked, residual risks will be monitored, new risks will be identified and the risk process itself gets attention and is subject to improvement.

In addition, in this process step, alternative strategies are chosen, contingency or fallback plans are executed, corrective actions are taken and the project management plan is modified.

Chapter 12
Project Procurement Management

As most projects need products, services or resources from outside the project team, then there will be a need to purchase them. Given the trends of outsourcing to ensure more competitive cost rates, as well as increasing project complexity which results in external input being frequently needed by specialists 'not available in-house', there is an increasing role for suppliers and partners. One can quickly conclude that a very simple fixed price contract is not the best starting point when dealing with complex arrangements where the contract scope is developed as the project progresses and the supplier's creativity is needed to get the best result within the given timeframe, budget and other constraints.

To deal with these situations effectively, one should apply Project Procurement Management.

Project Procurement Management consists of four processes:

1. Plan Procurements: to record purchasing decisions and to identify the approach and the potential sellers;
2. Conduct Procurements: to evaluate the seller responses, to select a seller and to sign the contract;
3. Administer Procurements: to manage the relationship with the seller and to monitor the seller's contract performance and make adjustments if needed;
4. Close Procurements: to complete the contract lifecycle for each procured item.

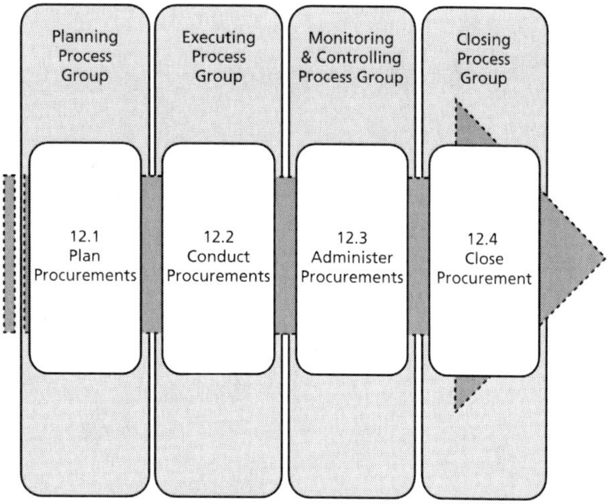

Figure 12.1 Overview of sections in Chapter 12 with the four Project Procurement Management processes

Since purchasing a product or a service always implies a legal binding agreement for both buyer and seller, you are advised to cover that in a formal contract.

Most organizations will have procurement policies and procedures that will define the rules to follow if you need to buy a third party product or service. In many cases it seems a good idea to involve the buying professionals of the organization to make sure the procurement process is executed in a professional way.

The procurement process actually manages the contract lifecycle. Deciding to buy (a part of) the project result instead of having it made by the project team could be triggered by a risk assessment, or a budgetary or time constraint.

If, for example, achieving a part of the project result is considered to be risky, buying that particular piece of work might mitigate the risk.

Every item to be purchased is subject to the four process steps outlined previously: from planning through to closing. And there are no exceptions.

Sellers are also known as contractors, subcontractors, vendors, service providers, or suppliers. A buyer can be called a client, customer, prime contractor, contractor, acquiring organization, governmental agency, service requestor, or purchaser. The seller's position during the contract lifecycle can change from bidder, via selected source, to contracted supplier.

For the purposes of this chapter we have assumed that the buyer is positioned in the project team and needs to buy items for the project; the seller is external to the project team. It is assumed that both seller and buyer develop a contractual relationship that needs to be managed.

12.1 Plan Procurements

Planning procurement for the project is about documenting the purchasing decisions, clarifying the procurement approach and identifying potential providers of the required goods or services.

It all starts with a buy-or-make decision. It clarifies which parts of the project result will be acquired externally and which parts are going to be created by the project team. The planning process not only focuses on the what, how and when of procurement, but also on the identification of potential sellers.

The planning of procurements will be based on the following inputs:

- The scope baseline;
- The project requirements;
- Cost estimates;
- The project schedule.

These four items define the boundaries of the project and will influence and will be influenced by any make-or-buy decision.

Any make-or-buy decision must be backed up by a solid make-or-buy analysis. This analysis assesses capabilities, budget and time constraints, and risks in order to answer the question: 'are we going to make it ourselves or are we going to purchase a 'solution'?

Buying products or services for a project requires dealing with technical, legal and commercial aspects. Involving a procurement specialist from the organization can be valuable to the project.

When it comes to contracts, there seem to be many variants but these all relate back to three basic types:

- Fixed price contracts;
- Cost reimbursable contracts;
- Time and material contracts.

These contract types actually define the level of risk sharing between the buyer and the seller. It is important to realize that the contract type of choice must serve the project's best interest and that is not necessarily a fixed price contract.

The procurement planning process must result in the following deliverables:

- The Procurement Management Plan that describes the way the project procurement process is going to be managed in terms of types of contracts to be used, how make-or-buy decisions will be handled, the application of procurement policies and procedures, the procurement metrics to be used etc.;
- Procurement statements of work that describe the procurement item in terms of specifications, required quantities, quality levels, delivery timelines etc.;
- Documented make-or-buy decisions;
- Procurement documents like Request For Information (RFI), Request For Proposal (RFP), Request For Quotation (RFQ);
- The selection criteria that will be used to rate the sellers' proposals.

12.2 Conduct Procurements

Conduct Procurements covers obtaining the responses of potential suppliers, selecting the preferred supplier and finally signing the contract with the selected supplier.

Based on the deliverables from the Procurement Planning Process, the team will evaluate the proposals from the interested suppliers and will finally select a supplier and come to an agreement by awarding the contract to that supplier.

Below you will find a generic list of the most important components of a contract:

- Statement of work;
- Timelines for delivery;
- Progress reporting;
- Roles and responsibilities;
- Location of performance;
- Pricing and payment terms;

- Place of delivery;
- Inspection and acceptance criteria;
- Warranty and product support;
- Limitation of liability;
- Change request handling;
- Termination and alternative dispute resolution mechanisms.

The process of procurement can be lengthy and may require quite some effort from the project team. The more complex or costly a required product or service is, the more time and effort it takes to finally award the contract.

Procurement negotiations can take some time before an agreement has been reached. Topics that should be covered are responsibilities, change authority, terms and conditions, governing law, proprietary rights, schedule payments and last but not least, price.

Reaching a final agreement by contract may eventually lead to updates of various components of the project management plan such as the cost, schedule and scope baseline and the procurement management plan.

Updates to the requirements documentation and the risk register might also be needed as a result of the agreed conditions in the contract.

12.3 Administer Procurements

After the contract is signed and execution has started, the project team need to:

- Manage the procurement relationships;
- Monitor the contract performance;
- Make adjustments if needed.

These activities are known as the Administer Procurements process. This process also includes integration of the appropriate project management processes such as:

- Direct and Manage Project Execution and Perform Integrated Change Control (see Chapter 4);
- Report Performance (see Chapter 10);
- Perform Quality Control (see Chapter 8);
- Monitor and Control Risks (see Chapter 11).

The financial component of this process kicks in once payments are due to the seller. Matching the payment terms with the seller's progress as contracted is a main concern. It is only too obvious that clear unambiguous targets should be stated in the contract to enable the progress measurement to be straightforward and not open to dispute.

It is important that the seller performs as contracted. If not, you might consider changes to the contract or even early termination. That is why it is important that such situations are covered in the contract. If a change to the contract is needed, you should follow the mutually agreed change process and use a change control system to have them properly administered.

Evaluating the seller's delivery can be done by a structured review, inspection or audit. Sometimes a simple performance report will do, though it will depend on the complexity of the contracted product or service.

Finally, the Administer Procurements process will lead to the following updates of the project management plan:

- Procurement plan updates in cases where change requests will impact the procurement process, project costs and/or the project schedule;
- Baseline schedule updates in cases where delays will impact overall project performance.

12.4 Close Procurements

All procurements need to be completed and closed. This process includes completing open claims, updating records with the final results and archiving them for future projects.

Contract closure can be prescribed by the terms and conditions in the contract. Usually open claims and early terminated contracts require special attention. They may require additional negotiations between buyer and seller to reach a mutual agreement on the procurement closure. Additional negotiations to settle all claims, disputes and issues are called negotiated settlements.

For a procurement to reach the status of closed, it is necessary to get a formal written statement from the seller that the contract has been completed. Requirements for formal closure are usually defined in the contract. All contract closure documents need to be filed as part of the procurement documentation.

The lessons learned and suggested improvements should also be documented for the benefit of future projects. A structured review of the entire Project Procurement Management process - a procurement audit – can contribute substantially to improved procurement in future projects.

Appendix A
Glossary

Definitions

Many of the words defined here have broader, and in some cases different, dictionary definitions.

The definitions use the following conventions:

- In some cases, a single glossary term consists of multiple words (e.g., risk response planning);
- When synonyms are included, no definition is given and the reader is directed to the preferred term (i.e., see preferred term);
- Related terms that are not synonyms are cross-referenced at the end of the definition (i.e., see also related term).

Acceptance Criteria. Those criteria, including performance requirements and essential conditions, which must be met before project deliverables are accepted.

Activity. A component of work performed during the course of a project.

Application Area. A category of projects that have common components significant in such projects, but are not needed or present in all projects. Application areas are usually defined in terms of either the product (i.e., by similar technologies or production methods) or the type of customer (i.e., internal versus external, government versus commercial) or industry sector (i.e., utilities, automotive, aerospace, information technologies, etc.). Application areas can overlap.

Assumptions. Assumptions are factors that, for planning purposes, are considered to be true, real, or certain without proof or demonstration.

Backward Pass. The calculation of late finish dates and late start dates for the uncompleted portions of all schedule activities. Determined by working backwards through the schedule network logic from the project's end date.

Baseline. An approved plan for a project, plus or minus approved changes. It is compared to actual performance to determine if performance is within acceptable variance thresholds. Generally refers to the current baseline, but may refer to the original or some other baseline. Usually used with a modifier (e.g., cost performance baseline, schedule baseline, performance measurement baseline, technical baseline).

Budget. The approved estimate for the project or any work breakdown structure component or any schedule activity. See also *estimate.*

Buyer. The acquirer of products, services, or results for an organization.

Change Control. Identifying, documenting, approving or rejecting, and controlling changes to the project baselines.

Change Request. Requests to expand or reduce the project scope, modify policies, processes, plans, or procedures, modify costs or budgets, or revise schedules.

Charter. See *project charter.*

Claim. A request, demand, or assertion of rights by a seller against a buyer, or vice versa, for consideration, compensation, or payment under the terms of a legally binding contract, such as for a disputed change.

Co-location. An organizational placement strategy where the project team members are physically located close to one another in order to improve communication, working relationships, and productivity.

Configuration Management System. A subsystem of the overall project management system. It is a collection of formal documented procedures used to apply technical and administrative direction and surveillance to: identify and document the functional and physical characteristics of a product, result, service, or component; control any changes to such characteristics; record and report each change and its implementation status; and support the audit of the products, results, or components to verify conformance to requirements. It includes the documentation, tracking systems, and defined approval levels necessary for authorizing and controlling changes.

Constraint. The state, quality, or sense of being restricted to a given course of action or inaction. An applicable restriction or limitation, either internal or external to a project, which will affect the performance of the project or a process. For example, a schedule constraint is any limitation or restraint placed on the project schedule that affects when a schedule activity can be scheduled and is usually in the form of fixed imposed dates.

Contingency. See *Reserve.*

Contingency Reserve. The amount of funds, budget, or time needed above the estimate to reduce the risk of overruns of project objectives to a level acceptable to the organization.

Control. Comparing actual performance with planned performance, analyzing variances, assessing trends to effect process improvements, evaluating possible alternatives, and recommending appropriate corrective action as needed.

Corrective Action. Documented direction for executing the project work to bring expected future performance of the project work in line with the project management plan.

Cost Performance Baseline. A specific version of the time-phased budget used to compare actual expenditures to planned expenditures to determine if preventive or corrective action is needed to meet the project objectives.

Crashing. A specific type of project schedule compression technique performed by taking action to decrease the total project schedule duration after analyzing a number of alternatives to determine how to get the maximum schedule duration compression for the least additional cost. Typical approaches for crashing a schedule include reducing schedule activity durations and increasing the assignment of resources on schedule activities. See also *fast tracking* and *schedule compression.*

Critical Path. Generally, but not always, the sequence of schedule activities that determines the duration of the project. It is the longest path through the project.

Defect. An imperfection or deficiency in a project component where that component does not meet its requirements or specifications and needs to be either repaired or replaced.

Deliverable. Any unique and verifiable product, result, or capability to perform a service that must be produced to complete a process, phase, or project. Often used more narrowly in reference to an external deliverable, which is a deliverable that is subject to approval by the project sponsor or customer. See also *Product.*

Earned Value (EV). The value of work performed expressed in terms of the approved budget assigned to that work for a schedule activity or work breakdown structure component. Also referred to as the budgeted cost of work performed (BCWP).

Earned Value Management (EVM). A management methodology for integrating scope, schedule, and resources, and for objectively measuring project performance and progress. Performance is measured by determining the budgeted cost of work performed (i.e., earned value) and comparing it to the actual cost of work performed (i.e., actual cost).

Effort. The number of labor units required to complete a schedule activity or work breakdown structure component. Usually expressed as staff hours, staff days, or staff weeks.

Enterprise Environmental Factors. Any or all external environmental factors and internal organizational environmental factors that surround or influence the project's success. These factors are from any or all of the enterprises involved in the project, and include organizational culture and structure, infrastructure, existing resources, commercial databases, market conditions, and project management software.

Estimate. A quantitative assessment of the likely amount or outcome. Usually applied to project costs, resources, effort, and durations and is usually preceded by a modifier (i.e., preliminary, conceptual, feasibility, order-of-magnitude, definitive). It should always include some indication of accuracy (e.g., ± x percent). See also *Budget.*

Execute. Directing, managing, performing, and accomplishing the project work, providing the deliverables, and providing work performance information.

Fast Tracking. A specific project schedule compression technique that changes network logic to overlap phases that would normally be done in sequence, such as the design phase and construction phase, or to perform schedule activities in parallel. See also *crashing* and *schedule compression*

Float. Also called slack. See *Total float* and *Free float.*

Forecast. An estimate or prediction of conditions and events in the project's future based on information and knowledge available at the time of the forecast. The information is based on the project's past performance and expected future performance, and includes information that could impact the project in the future, such as estimate at completion and estimate to complete.

Forward Pass. The calculation of the early start and early finish dates for the uncompleted portions of all network activities. See also *Backward pass.*

Free Float. The amount of time that a schedule activity can be delayed without delaying the early start date of any immediately following schedule activities. See also *total float.*

Functional Manager. Someone with management authority over an organizational unit within a functional organization. The manager of any group that actually makes a product or performs a service. Sometimes called a line manager.

Functional Organization. A hierarchical organization where each employee has one clear superior, and staff are grouped by areas of specialization and managed by a person with expertise in that area.

Gantt Chart. A graphic display of schedule-related information. In the typical bar chart, schedule activities or work breakdown structure components are listed down the left side of the chart, dates are shown across the top, and activity durations are shown as date-placed horizontal bars.

Grade. A category or rank used to distinguish items that have the same functional use (e.g., "hammer"), but do not share the same requirements for quality (e.g., different hammers may need to withstand different amounts of force).

Imposed Date. A fixed date imposed on a schedule activity or schedule milestone, usually in the form of a "start no earlier than" and "finish no later than" date.

Issue. A point or matter in question or in dispute, or a point or matter that is not settled and is under discussion or over which there are opposing views or disagreements.

Lessons Learned. The learning gained from the process of performing the project. Lessons learned may be identified at any point. Also considered a project record, to be included in the lessons learned knowledge base.

Matrix Organization. Any organizational structure in which the project manager shares responsibility with the functional managers for assigning priorities and for directing the work of persons assigned to the project.

Methodology. A system of practices, techniques, procedures, and rules used by those who work in a discipline.

Milestone. A significant point or event in the project.

Objective. Something toward which work is to be directed, a strategic position to be attained, or a purpose to be achieved, a result to be obtained, a product to be produced, or a service to be performed.

Opportunity. A condition or situation favorable to the project, a positive set of circumstances, a positive set of events, a risk that will have a positive impact on project objectives, or a possibility for positive changes. Contrast with *threat*.

Pareto Chart. A histogram, ordered by frequency of occurrence, that shows how many results were generated by each identified cause.

Performance Measurement Baseline. An approved integrated scope-schedule-cost plan for the project work against which project execution is compared to measure and manage performance. Technical and quality parameters may also be included.

Performance Reports. Documents and presentations that provide organized and summarized work performance information, earned value management parameters and calculations, and analyses of project work progress and status.

Performing Organization. The enterprise whose personnel are most directly involved in doing the work of the project.

Portfolio. A collection of projects or programs and other work that are grouped together to facilitate effective management of that work to meet strategic business objectives. The projects or programs of the portfolio may not necessarily be interdependent or directly related.

Portfolio Management. The centralized management of one or more portfolios, which includes identifying, prioritizing, authorizing, managing, and controlling projects, programs, and other related work, to achieve specific strategic business objectives.

Preventive Action. A documented direction to perform an activity that can reduce the probability of negative consequences associated with project risks.

Product. An artifact that is produced, is quantifiable, and can be either an end item in itself or a component item. Additional words for products are material and goods. Contrast with *result*. See also *Deliverable*.

Product Life Cycle. A collection of generally sequential, non-overlapping product phases whose name and number are determined by the manufacturing and control needs of the organization. The last product life cycle phase for a product is generally the product's retirement. Generally, a project life cycle is contained within one or more product life cycles.

Product Scope. The features and functions that characterize a product, service, or result.

Program. A group of related projects managed in a coordinated way to obtain benefits and control not available from managing them individually. Programs may include elements of related work outside of the scope of the discrete projects in the program.

Program Management. The centralized coordinated management of a program to achieve the program's strategic objectives and benefits.

Project. A temporary endeavor undertaken to create a unique product, service, or result.

Project Charter. A document issued by the project initiator or sponsor that formally authorizes the existence of a project, and provides the project manager with the authority to apply organizational resources to project activities.

Project Life Cycle. A collection of generally sequential project phases whose name and number are determined by the control needs of the organization or organizations involved in the project. A life cycle can be documented with a methodology.

Project Management. The application of knowledge, skills, tools, and techniques to project activities to meet the project requirements.

Project Management Body of Knowledge. An inclusive term that describes the sum of knowledge within the profession of project management. As with other professions, such as law, medicine, and accounting, the body of knowledge rests with the practitioners and academics that apply and advance it. The complete project management body of knowledge includes proven traditional practices that are widely applied and innovative practices that are emerging in the profession. The body of knowledge includes both published and unpublished materials. This body of knowledge is constantly evolving. PMI's *PMBOK® Guide* identifies that subset of the project management body of knowledge that is generally recognized as good practice.

Project Management Knowledge Area. An identified area of project management defined by its knowledge requirements and described in terms of its component processes, practices, inputs, outputs, tools, and techniques.

Project Management Office (PMO). An organizational body or entity assigned various responsibilities related to the centralized and coordinated management of those projects under its domain.

The responsibilities of a PMO can range from providing project management support functions to actually being responsible for the direct management of a project.

Project Management Plan. A formal, approved document that defines how the project is executed, monitored, and controlled. It may be a summary or detailed and may be composed of one or more subsidiary management plans and other planning documents.

Project Management Team. The members of the project team who are directly involved in project management activities. On some smaller projects, the project management team may include virtually all of the project team members.

Project Manager (PM). The person assigned by the performing organization to achieve the project objectives.

Project Phase. A collection of logically related project activities, usually culminating in the completion of a major deliverable. Project phases are mainly completed sequentially, but can overlap in some project situations. A project phase is a component of a project life cycle. A project phase is not a project management process group.

Project Scope. The work that must be performed to deliver a product, service, or result with the specified features and functions.

Projectized Organization. Any organizational structure in which the project manager has full authority to assign priorities, apply resources, and direct the work of persons assigned to the project.

Quality. The degree to which a set of inherent characteristics fulfills requirements.

Regulation. Requirements imposed by a governmental body. These requirements can establish product, process, or service characteristics, including applicable administrative provisions that have government-mandated compliance.

Request for Information (RFI). A type of procurement document whereby the buyer requests a potential seller to provide various pieces of information related to a product or service or seller capability.

Request for Proposal (RFP). A type of procurement document used to request proposals from prospective sellers of products or services. In some application areas, it may have a narrower or more specific meaning.

Request for Quotation (RFQ). A type of procurement document used to request price quotations from prospective sellers of common or standard products or services. Sometimes used in place of request for proposal and in some application areas, it may have a narrower or more specific meaning.

Requirement. A condition or capability that must be met or possessed by a system, product, service, result, or component to satisfy a contract, standard, specification, or other formally imposed document. Requirements include the quantified and documented needs, wants, and expectations of the sponsor, customer, and other stakeholders.

Reserve. A provision in the project management plan to mitigate cost and/or schedule risk. Often used with a modifier (e.g., management reserve, contingency reserve) to provide further detail on what types of risk are meant to be mitigated.

Residual Risk. A risk that remains after risk responses have been implemented.

Resource. Skilled human resources (specific disciplines either individually or in crews or teams), equipment, services, supplies, commodities, material, budgets, or funds.

Risk. An uncertain event or condition that, if it occurs, has a positive or negative effect on a project's objectives.

Risk Register. The document containing the results of the qualitative risk analysis, quantitative risk analysis, and risk response planning. The risk register details all identified risks, including description, category, cause, probability of occurring, impact(s) on objectives, proposed responses, owners, and current status.

Risk Tolerance. The degree, amount, or volume of risk that an organization or individual will withstand.

Schedule Baseline. A specific version of the schedule model used to compare actual results to the plan to determine if preventive or corrective action is needed to meet the project objectives.

Schedule Compression. Shortening the project schedule duration without reducing the project scope. See also *crashing* and *fast tracking*.

Scope. The sum of the products, services, and results to be provided as a project. See also *Project scope* and *Product scope*.

Scope Baseline. An approved specific version of the detailed scope statement, work breakdown structure (WBS), and its associated WBS dictionary.

Scope Change. Any change to the project scope. A scope change almost always requires an adjustment to the project cost or schedule.

Scope Creep. Adding features and functionality (project scope) without addressing the effects on time, costs, and resources, or without customer approval.

Secondary Risk. A risk that arises as a direct result of implementing a risk response.

Seller. A provider or supplier of products, services, or results to an organization.

Slack. Also called float. See *Total float* and *Free float*.

Specification. A document that specifies, in a complete, precise, verifiable manner, the requirements, design, behavior, or other characteristics of a system, component, product, result, or service and, often, the procedures for determining whether these provisions have been satisfied. Examples are: requirement specification, design specification, product specification, and test specification.

Sponsor. The person or group that provides the financial resources, in cash or in kind, for the project.

Staffing Management Plan. The document that describes when and how human resource requirements will be met. It is contained in, or is a subsidiary plan of, the human resource plan.

Stakeholder. Person or organization (e.g., customer, sponsor, performing organization, or the public) that is actively involved in the project, or whose interests may be positively or negatively affected by execution or completion of the project. A stakeholder may also exert influence over the project and its deliverables.

Standard. A document that provides, for common and repeated use, rules, guidelines, or characteristics for activities or their results, aimed at the achievement of the optimum degree of order in a given context.

Statement of Work (SOW). A narrative description of products, services, or results to be supplied.

Strengths, Weaknesses, Opportunities, and Threats (SWOT) Analysis. This information gathering technique examines the project from the perspective of each project's strengths, weaknesses, opportunities, and threats to increase the breadth of the risks considered by risk management.

Template. A partially complete document in a predefined format that provides a defined structure for collecting, organizing, and presenting information and data.

Threat. A condition or situation unfavorable to the project, a negative set of circumstances, a negative set of events, a risk that will have a negative impact on a project objective if it occurs, or a possibility for negative changes. Contrast with *Opportunity*.

Total Float. The total amount of time that a schedule activity may be delayed from its early start date without delaying the project finish date, or violating a schedule constraint. Calculated using the critical path method technique and determining the difference between the early finish dates and late finish dates. See also *Free float*.

Validation. The assurance that a product, service, or system meets the needs of the customer and other identified stakeholders. It often involves acceptance and suitability with external customers. Contrast with *Verification*.

Value Engineering. An approach used to optimize project life cycle costs, save time, increase profits, improve quality, expand market share, solve problems, and/or use resources more effectively.

Variance. A quantifiable deviation, departure, or divergence away from a known baseline or expected value.

Verification. The evaluation of whether or not a product, service, or system complies with a regulation, requirement, specification, or imposed condition. It is often an internal process. Contrast with validation.

Virtual Team. A group of persons with a shared objective who fulfill their roles with little or no time spent meeting face to face. Various forms of technology are often used to facilitate communication among team members. Virtual teams can be comprised of persons separated by great distances.

Work Breakdown Structure (WBS). A deliverable-oriented hierarchical decomposition of the work to be executed by the project team to accomplish the project objectives and create the required deliverables. It organizes and defines the total scope of the project.

Work Package. A deliverable or project work component at the lowest level of each branch of the work breakdown structure.

Workaround. A response to a negative risk that has occurred. Distinguished from contingency plan in that a workaround is not planned in advance of the occurrence of the risk event.

About the authors

Paul Snijders, PMP, started his profesional career in 1989 as a project manager in information technology. During the Nineties Paul managed IT projects in logistics, finance, graphic arts industry and oil & gas. He worked as a project manager for companies like KPN, Hewlett-Packard and Atos-Origin, later on as an independent project manager and worked ever since in the ERP arena with a strong focus on logistics and HR.
Paul is a longtime certified project manager.
In 1997 he successfully applied for the Level B project management certificate from the renowned International Project Management Association (IPMA).
Although a supporter of the school of eclectic project management, Paul is impressed by the richness of the PRINCE2 project management methodology. In 2001 he got his Prince 2 Practitioner certificate.
In search for excellence, Paul came across the Project Management Institute and their project management standard as captured in the Project Management Body of Knowledge (PMBoK). In 2005 he got his Project Management Professional (*PMBOK® Guide*) certificate.
Since 1999 Paul delivers his Project Management Fundamentals training to business and IT professionals. Hundreds of participants have enjoyed Paul's style of training delivery: high speed, humorous and to-the-point.
Paul will guide you through the project management landscape. Beyond methodologies, he will teach you the tricks of the trade that really work and eventually will make the difference between success and failure.
Lately Paul performs as motivational speaker for various audiences on hot topics in project management. Paul's drive is to get his message across to whoever want to hear it: only competent project managers will succeed in delivering projects that satisfy its customers and stakeholders.

Thomas Wuttke, PMP, PMI-RMP, PMI-ACP, CSM, has a degree in Computer Science from the University of Applied Sciences in Karlsruhe, Germany and has worked for more than 20 years on large IT integration projects in both the public and commercial sectors. He has intensive project and program management experience and has been a general manager and an executive sponsor. Thomas was International Partner at the Belgium headquarters of Threon Europe after his own project management consulting firm, *9:pm*, merged 2006 with the Threon group. In 1996 Thomas passed the IPMA level B certification, achieved the PMP credential and was one of the first PMI certified project managers in Germany. He also served as a Director on PMI's *Certification Board Center Board of Directors* and was the Chapter president of the PMI Munich Chapter for 5 years. Thomas pioneered the German translation of the *PMBOK® Guides* before the PMI standard was available in its final form with 12 languages. He has published several articles and is the lead author of *Das PMP-Examen*, a book on preparing for the PMP@ Exam.
Thomas is a renowned and inspirational trainer, consultant, coach and speaker with assignments across Europe, China, Korea, Japan, India, Brazil and the United States. His favorite topics are aligning strategy with projects and programs, improving organizational maturity, introducing real and practical risk management, riding the waves of the cultural challenge and creating project management career ladders.
Thomas is married, has three children and lives in the vicinity of Munich where he enjoys Bavarian mentality, sailing and mountaineering.

Anton Zandhuis, PMP, started his professional career in 1989 with the Netherlands Organization for Applied Scientific Research (TNO). He worked for large international research projects, focusing on the financial, business and project management aspects. He then moved to Arthur Andersen, managing ERP implementation projects and later Deloitte, becoming manager of the ICT project managers, implementing project, program and portfolio good practices as well as developing and

implementing the ICT-Business alignment. In 2006 he joined Threon as Executive partner a renowned European business partner for implementing excellence in project management.
Anton has a real passion for the project management profession, as it's all about people and the initiation and implementation of changes.
Next to his continuous development in the project management profession, he was one of the co-founders of the PMI Netherlands Chapter (founded in 2000 - honorary member), served as Board member for several years in different roles, managed the 5th PMI Benelux day, and became Board member of the Program Board Dutch publications of the PMI Netherlands Chapter. He took part in the review team of the first Dutch translation of the *PMBOK® Guide* 3rd edition (published in 2006) and managed the Dutch translation of the *PMBOK® Guide* 4th edition (published in May 2009). He is a certified PMP as well as Prince 2 Practitioner.
Currently Anton delivers delivers project, program and portfolio management coaching, consultancy and training to organizations in several application areas (ICT, Manufacturing, Banking, ...) for an international audience. He takes a pragmatic view, good practices and a Lifecycle based approach, applies it with creativity and humor - given the specific business and peoples' needs and the job at hand – and with a high focus on 'quick value delivery' as well as 'gradual competency growth'. Anton's drive is to share his enthusiasm for the project management profession. He believes that, when applied pragmatically, it leads to motivated, more focused, and effective teams, thus bringing out the best of people, and with successful project and program delivery and better and sustainable business results as an outcome.
Anton is married, has two children and lives in Delft where he enjoys cooking with family and friends and riding his motorbike.

Made in United States
North Haven, CT
04 November 2026

21763082R00087